Summer Savory Mustard Marinade
(makes approximately 3 cups)

1/3 cup Dijon-style (or grainy) mustard
2 tablespoons minced shallots
2 cloves minced garlic
2 cups high-quality olive oil
2/3 cup red wine vinegar
2–3 tablespoons finely
chopped summer savory
salt to taste

Seedless
green
grapes

$3.99
Per
Pound
CRUNCHY!

CE
APES
CH!!

OBE
APES
3.99
LB

HYD
MED
$5.9

WASHINGTON
DANJOU
PEARS
$1.99
LB

JUMBO
ASIAN P
$3

WYNNE

PURE FLAVOR

125 FRESH ALL-AMERICAN RECIPES

FROM THE PACIFIC NORTHWEST

KURT BEECHER DAMMEIER

WITH LAURA HOLMES HADDAD

Foreword by Tom Douglas ■ Photographs by Maren Caruso

CLARKSON POTTER/PUBLISHERS

NEW YORK

Copyright © 2007 by Sugar Mountain Cookbooks LLC
Foreword copyright © 2007 by Tom Douglas
Photographs © 2007 by Maren Caruso

Published in the United States by Clarkson Potter/Publishers, an imprint of the
Crown Publishing Group, a division of Random House, Inc., New York.
www.crownpublishing.com
www.clarksonpotter.com

Clarkson N. Potter is a trademark and Potter and colophon are registered trademarks
of Random House, Inc.

Library of Congress Cataloging-in-Publication Data
Dammeier, Kurt Beecher.
   Pure flavor: 125 fresh all-American recipes from the Pacific Northwest /
Kurt Beecher Dammeier, with Laura Holmes Haddad.
       p.   cm.
   Includes index.
1. Cookery, American—Pacific Northwest style.   I. Haddad, Laura Holmes.   II. Title.
TX715.2.P32D36   2007
641.59795—dc22   2006028773

ISBN 978-0-307-34642-1

Printed in China

Design by Jane Treuhaft

10   9   8   7   6   5   4   3   2   1

FIRST EDITION

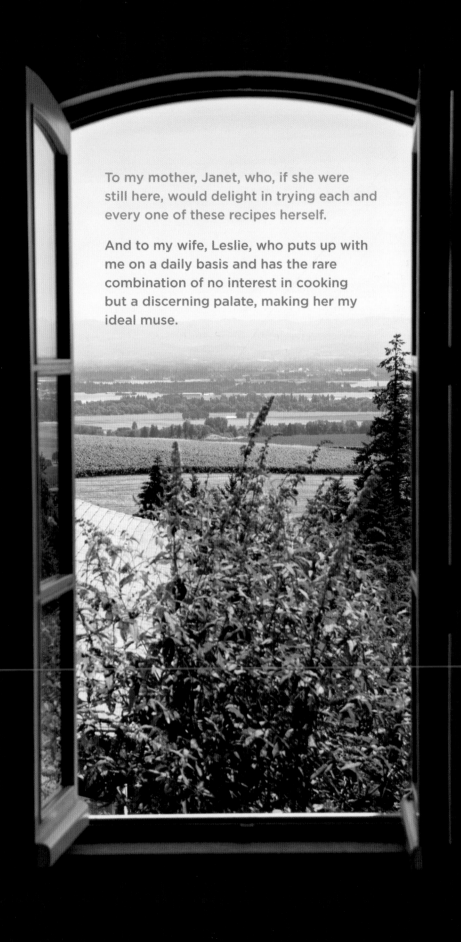

To my mother, Janet, who, if she were still here, would delight in trying each and every one of these recipes herself.

And to my wife, Leslie, who puts up with me on a daily basis and has the rare combination of no interest in cooking but a discerning palate, making her my ideal muse.

CONTENTS

FOREWORD

KURT DAMMEIER IS A MODERN-DAY RENAISSANCE MAN, and that might be an understatement. He's as comfortable as a fund manager handling stocks and bonds, a real estate agent handling complex land swaps, a top-notch skier gliding down the slopes of Baldy Mountain in Sun Valley, or a superb golfer working on his handicap at any of Seattle's golf courses. But deep down, Kurt is really a food man, I think, because he's happiest of all culling curds for his Beecher's Flagship cheese.

When Kurt starts something, he doesn't do it halfway. He dives in headfirst. It's fitting that Kurt's swan dive landed him smack dab in the middle of the Pike Place Market, the gastronomic heart and soul of Seattle. With a keen sensibility, Kurt identified a missing link in a market filled with cheese shops but not a single cheese artisan—and he set out to fill that gap. The result is Beecher's Handmade Cheese, a bright light-filled shop with hardwood floors and big plate-glass windows where you can sample fresh cheese curds, pick up a cup of macaroni and cheese, and, best of all, watch the cheesemaker at work making cheese in big open vats right before your eyes.

Kurt's vision doesn't stop at the ordinary. He didn't just want to make cheese; he wanted to find a source of locally produced milk that's free of synthetic hormones. When he fulfilled that goal, consistent supply became a problem, so Kurt bought his own cows—a single herd of about two hundred cows—to make sure they could roam and graze freely and would be fed high-quality feed.

Kurt and his wife, Leslie, have three young sons in grade school, Max, Bennett, and Liam. They all quickly realized the horrible state of cafeteria meals in the local schools. Refusing to sit on their hands, Kurt and Leslie developed and funded "Pure Food Kids: A Recipe for Healthy Eating" to enrich the curriculum of local schools and preach the gospel of pure food and flavor.

Pure Flavor is a great look at what's happening right now, with straightforward, commonsense advice about what *organic* means, what *free range* means, what fair trade coffee is—it's clearly explained right here. We all should seek out "pure flavors" by buying what's local, supporting organic farms and ranchers, insisting on better product labeling, and using our dollars to vote for no additives, no hormones, no artificial colorings or preservatives (and if Kurt had his way, *no* Cheetos!).

The recipes in *Pure Flavor* form a comprehensive guide to cooking in this new century: simple, modern food that's accessible and fun. A couple of recipes to try right away: the addictive, rich, creamy "World's Best" Mac and Cheese and the Strawberry Shortcake with Fromage Blanc Whipped Cream. Of course the fromage blanc to use here is Beecher's Honey Blank Slate!

—TOM DOUGLAS
Seattle

INTRODUCTION

PURE FLAVOR IS THE ESSENCE OF EVERYTHING WE EAT—food that tastes like it's supposed to and reflects the natural rhythm of the seasons. This is especially true in the Pacific Northwest, where we are surrounded by an endless bounty from our farms, mountains, rivers, and the Pacific Ocean. Nowadays, with food often packed, shipped, ripened in a warehouse, or flown in from abroad, the true, pure flavor of food can get lost somewhere along the way.

Living in the Pacific Northwest makes you pay attention to your food. Whether it's a rich, crunchy hazelnut from Oregon, a plump blueberry from the mountains of Washington, or fresh salmon from Puget Sound, our fantastic local foods make shopping, cooking, and eating more a joy than a chore. My culinary approach is to source great raw material and then prepare it in a way that lets the ingredients shine through. This is something anyone can do in almost any region of the country. In local markets and farmer's markets, you can find food that has traveled from the field to the farm to the consumer, with just a brief stop in between.

Searching out pure flavor in farm-fresh foods is not only a healthy way to eat but also an easier way to prepare a meal. When you buy fantastic, natural ingredients, it takes less effort to make their flavors sing. A pinch of salt, a dash of pepper, and most meat, fish, and vegetables come to life.

If we're lucky, we experienced pure flavor when we were young, grabbing a handful of berries from a wild blackberry bush or sneaking an apple from a low-hanging branch in the neighbor's yard. For me, it was cheese that brought me to pure flavor. My father's parents always had a cheese board in the kitchen piled high with local cheeses, which we devoured on Sunday afternoons. There wasn't a holiday at Grandma's house that didn't feature big blocks of local Cheddar. My

mother's mother used to tell me about the wheels of Stilton my Scottish great-grandfather Beecher would bring home. If I close my eyes, I can still taste those amazing flavors. It's no wonder I'm now a cheese guy.

This obsession—I would say passion—for pure flavor has driven me to live out what was once just a dream. After graduating from college, all I wanted to do was work in food, but I joined my family's printing business instead. Years later we sold the business, and I was free to pursue my passion—which started, as it has for many people in this business, in Mom's kitchen. My mother, Janet, cooked for us every night in my hometown of Tacoma, Washington. She entertained her friends on the weekends, and I often sat in the kitchen watching her slice onions, peel potatoes, or sauté pork chops.

Where my style diverges from my mother's is that while she followed recipes to the letter, I am always looking for ways to change them. Food is like music to me. It's rare that I hear a song and don't want to fine-tune it by bringing up the guitar or repeating the refrain one more time. To me, food isn't static, and even though these recipes are favorites with our customers, have been tested by home cooks, and will bring fresh flavors to your dinner table, I encourage you to add your own touches. Find what looks best in your region and tweak these recipes a little. I even give you sug-

gestions for other flavor combinations that might work. In fact, many of the recipes have elements that can be used interchangeably, and many can be made ahead to make mealtimes a little easier and a lot more enjoyable.

Eating seasonally is an important element to this approach. Cherries just taste better in the summer, apples are crisp and delicious in the fall, and no matter where you live and what food you have access to, you can still eat seasonally. I often provide substitution suggestions for ingredients, but the best ingredient will always be the one that was grown down the road from your house.

Cheese is a great starting point for understanding pure flavor. While I'm a big fan of local cheeses, make no mistake, cheese really can travel well and is an easy way to bring pure flavor to your table, as long as you shy away from the flavorless, mass-produced, vacuum-packed slices found in your supermarket's deli case. Walk up to any cheese counter and buy the most intriguing

cheese you see, whether it's familiar or not. It's hard to go wrong, and you will learn while you taste. Cow's, sheep's, or goat's milk—take a moment to explore the different flavors, aromas, and stories that reveal themselves in every bite. What the animal ate, where the farm is—these elements will instantly come alive. Take a risk and treat it as an adventure.

Cheese can also be used as a seasoning as much as a main ingredient in a dish. Incorporating cheese into a recipe is an easy task due to its *umami* characteristics. (*Umami* is the Japanese word for "savory," a taste that encompasses the entire mouth. It is becoming accepted as a fifth taste, in addition to bitter, sweet, salty, and sour.) Because of this, I often use cheese to give a dish a rounder, richer flavor, almost as a background ingredient. This pumps up the flavor naturally without the need for the artificial additives found in many packaged foods.

Making the leap from cheese lover to cheese

producer happened faster than I imagined. I always wondered why my home state of Washington didn't have its own great cheese tradition, like Wisconsin or Vermont. The city of Seattle embraces artisanal products and prides itself on supporting food entrepreneurs, so I knew the residents would rally to the cause. I also knew the climate and soil in Washington State would provide the necessary raw material for great milk, the most important element in any cheese. The Pacific Northwest is a nurturing place to start a food business because the culture upholds a standard of excellence while tolerating experimentation.

When a retail space opened up at Pike Place Market, all of the pieces came together. Beecher's Handmade Cheese opened its doors in 2003, and so far it has been quite a ride. Many of our customers get their first view of how food travels from the animal to the dinner table in our store,

which features stories about the local dairies we work with and displays cheesemaking in progress. It's an ideal way of getting people to think about the provenance of the food they eat. Kids and adults alike press their noses to the store windows to watch cheese being made in the shiny metal vats and delight in sampling our selection of regional cheeses from around the United States. We set out to make great cheese, but we do that and more: We bring pure flavors and healthy eating to our customers.

And this passion for pure flavor isn't limited to cheese. I bought Pasta & Co from founders Marcella and Harvey Rosene in 2000, and there I learned my first lessons in the food business. With gourmet, all-natural prepared food, fresh bread, homemade sauces, and, of course, pasta, the stores have become an important part of the Seattle neighborhoods.

In 2006 we opened the doors to Bennett's Pure Food Bistro, a full-service restaurant in my neighborhood of Mercer Island, located just outside of Seattle. Continuing our passion for food with integrity, the restaurant features dishes made with fresh, local, and seasonal ingredients that celebrate the region.

Someone once described me as a person who doesn't want to do things the way they've been done before, and I suppose that's an accurate description. I hope you can take something from this book that helps you understand more about pure flavor, about the bounty in your own backyard, as well as prepare a really great meal—or three.

Here's to healthy eating.

—KURT BEECHER DAMMEIER
Seattle

SALAD SPECIAL

Spring Greens with fresh
radishes, sweet onion; tender peas
tossed with a lemon poppyseed
dressing - garnished with roasted
Yakima asparagus, Oregon hazelnuts
; shaved Grana Padano cheese
$ 7.95

Soups
THAI PEANUT w/ TOFU
(VEGETARIAN)
FRENCH ONION

SOUPS & SANDWICHES

SPICED BUTTERNUT SQUASH SOUP

WHITE BEAN SOUP WITH FRESH SAGE

ONE-HOUR CHICKEN SOUP FROM SCRATCH

FRENCH ONION SOUP

TOMATO-CHEDDAR SOUP

CRAB AND LEEK CHOWDER

TOASTED TOMATO-BASIL SANDWICH

TOASTED BRIE AND SWEET THAI CHILI SAUCE SANDWICH

TOASTED PROSCIUTTO, CHEDDAR, AND APPLE SANDWICH

CORNMEAL-CRUSTED OYSTER SANDWICH

SPICED BUTTERNUT SQUASH SOUP

MAKES 10 CUPS; SERVES 6 TO 8

THE INTENSE FLAVOR OF AUTUMN SQUASH is magnified when turned into a smooth, luscious soup. Adding yams provides even more depth of flavor, and Middle Eastern spices keep the sweetness in check.

5 tablespoons unsalted butter

2 tablespoons neutral-flavored cooking oil, such as canola or soybean

1 large yellow onion, diced

1 teaspoon ground cumin

1 teaspoon ground coriander

1³/₄ pounds butternut squash (1 large squash), peeled, seeded, and sliced

1¹/₂ pounds yams, peeled and sliced

2¹/₂ teaspoons kosher salt, or more to taste

Pinch of cayenne pepper

¹/₄ teaspoon nutmeg

¹/₄ teaspoon freshly ground black pepper, or more to taste

³/₄ cup sliced almonds

2 tablespoons thinly sliced fresh sage

In a heavy-bottomed 8-quart stockpot, heat 1 tablespoon of the butter and the oil over medium-high heat. Add the onion and cook, stirring frequently, until soft but not browned, about 4 minutes. Stir in the cumin and coriander and cook for 1 minute.

Add the butternut squash, yams, 8 cups water, and salt. Simmer for 35 to 40 minutes, or until the vegetables are very soft. Using an immersion blender, puree the soup until smooth. Alternatively, pour the mixture into a food processor or blender and return it to the pot after processing.

Stir in the cayenne pepper, nutmeg, and black pepper. Taste for seasoning and add additional salt, cayenne pepper, nutmeg, or black pepper as needed.

For the topping, melt the remaining 4 tablespoons butter in a small skillet over medium heat. Add the almonds and sauté until light golden brown, stirring frequently. Add the sage and continue to stir for 1 minute, or until the almonds are golden brown and the sage is fragrant. Remove the topping to a bowl to cool.

To serve, garnish each bowl of soup with 1¹/₂ tablespoons of the topping.

MAKE AHEAD The soup will keep, covered, in the refrigerator for up to 5 days or in the freezer for up to 6 months. Gently reheat over low heat, stirring frequently to avoid burning.

WHITE BEAN SOUP
with Fresh Sage

MAKES 4 CUPS; SERVES 2 TO 4

WHEN COLD WEATHER SETTLES IN, it's time for this rich soup. Bacon adds even deeper flavor to the classic Italian white beans and sage combination. Using nitrate-free bacon is the best option, for both flavor and health reasons, and it's becoming more widely available.

1 tablespoon unsalted butter

2 tablespoons roughly chopped fresh sage

4 ounces bacon (about 4 strips), diced

About 2 tablespoons extra-virgin olive oil

11 large garlic cloves, peeled

1 celery rib, thinly sliced

1 medium yellow onion, diced

1/2 cup white wine

2 cups Chicken Stock (page 230) or low-sodium store-bought chicken broth

2 15-ounce cans Great Northern beans, drained and rinsed in cold water

3 tablespoons finely chopped, drained sun-dried tomatoes in oil

1 tablespoon chopped green olives

2 ounces Parmesan or other hard cheese, grated (1/2 cup)

1/2 teaspoon kosher salt

1/4 teaspoon freshly ground black pepper

Melt the butter in a small skillet over medium-high heat. Cook until the butter browns, about 2 minutes. Add the sage and sauté for 30 seconds. Set aside.

Heat a 4-quart saucepan over medium heat. Add the bacon and sauté for 6 minutes or until crisp and brown. Remove the bacon with a slotted spoon to a small bowl, leaving the bacon fat in the pan. Return the pan to medium heat.

Add enough olive oil to the bacon fat to make about 4 tablespoons total. Add the garlic cloves and stir until they are fully coated. Cook the garlic until it just begins to brown, stirring frequently to prevent burning, about 5 minutes. With a slotted spoon, remove the garlic to the bowl with the bacon.

Add the celery and onion to the pan and sauté over medium-high heat for 2 minutes, until the vegetables are soft and translucent but not brown. Add the wine, stir, and cook for 2 to 3 minutes, or until the wine has nearly evaporated. Add the stock, beans, bacon, garlic, half of the sage, 1 tablespoon of the sun-dried tomatoes, 1/2 tablespoon of the olives, and the cheese, salt, and pepper. Blend the mixture briefly with an immersion blender, just until the garlic is chopped. (The texture should be chunky.) Alternatively, puree the mixture in a food processor or blender, returning the soup to the pan after processing.

Bring to a boil, and then simmer on low heat for 10 minutes.

Serve the soup garnished with the remaining sage, sun-dried tomatoes, and olives.

MAKE AHEAD The soup may be refrigerated for 4 days or frozen for up to 3 months.

ONE-HOUR CHICKEN SOUP
from Scratch

MAKES ABOUT 6 CUPS; SERVES 4

WHILE SOME PEOPLE THINK IT'S TOO HARD or takes too much time to make home-made chicken soup, this recipe was originally created for a kids' cooking class to illustrate how easy it is to make pure foods instead of opening up a can. You don't need many ingredients or much time; take 20 minutes to prep and 35 minutes to simmer, and within an hour you've got a healthy, flavorful soup to enjoy all week.

1 to 2 tablespoons extra-virgin olive oil
1 pound boneless, skinless chicken thighs
1½ teaspoons kosher salt
3 celery ribs, chopped
1 large carrot, chopped
½ medium yellow onion, roughly chopped

1 tablespoon House Herbs (page 233) or other dried Italian herb blend
3 garlic cloves, roughly chopped
½ cup short pasta, such as small elbow macaroni or rotini
2 dashes Tabasco or other hot sauce

Heat 1 tablespoon of the oil in a stockpot or large pot over high heat. Cut the chicken thighs into 1-inch pieces. Season the chicken with ½ teaspoon of the salt and add it to the pot. Cook the chicken for 4 minutes without stirring, or until it is browned. Flip the chicken and cook for an additional 3 to 4 minutes, or until the second side is browned. (Browning the chicken pieces well adds richness and color to the soup.) Set the chicken aside in a separate bowl, leaving as much fat as possible in the pot. If no fat is left, add the additional tablespoon olive oil.

Add the celery, carrots, onion, and herbs to the pot and cook over medium heat for 5 minutes, stirring occasionally, until the carrots are slightly soft. Add the garlic and cook for 1 minute. While stirring, scrape any brown bits off the bottom of the pot and incorporate them with the vegetables.

Return the chicken and any juices that have accumulated in the bowl to the pot. Add 5 cups water and stir. Bring the soup to a boil over high heat, and then reduce the heat to low. If any scum has formed on the top, skim it off. Simmer the soup for 15 minutes, and then stir in the pasta. Simmer for an additional 15 minutes. If the pasta is not done, continue simmering until the pasta is fully cooked.

Stir in the hot sauce and remaining teaspoon salt and serve.

MAKE AHEAD The soup will keep, covered, in the refrigerator for up to 4 days or in the freezer for up to 3 months.

FRENCH ONION SOUP

MAKES 6 CUPS; SERVES 4

THE RICH FLAVORS OF CLASSIC FRENCH ONION SOUP are especially comforting on a cold, gray day. The original recipe is lightened here by substituting chicken for beef stock. The croutons are the grand finale, and making them yourself is a snap; simply top sliced bread with cheese, bake on a baking sheet at 350°F. until golden brown, and cut into cubes. If possible, use homemade Chicken Stock (page 230) in this soup; the flavor is incomparable.

4 tablespoons ($\frac{1}{2}$ stick) unsalted butter

4 medium yellow onions, sliced

3 tablespoons all-purpose flour

6 cups Chicken Stock (page 230) or store-bought low-sodium chicken broth

$\frac{1}{4}$ cup white wine

1 tablespoon red wine vinegar

1 teaspoon kosher salt, or more to taste

$\frac{1}{2}$ teaspoon freshly ground black pepper, or more to taste

$\frac{1}{4}$ teaspoon fresh thyme

Semihard cheese, such as Gruyère (page 23), grated, for garnish (optional)

Croutons, for garnish (optional; see headnote)

In a large, deep skillet over medium-high heat, melt 3 tablespoons of the butter. Add the onions and stir until they are fully coated. Cook for 10 minutes, stirring frequently, until the onions are softened. Reduce the heat to medium-low and continue to cook until the onions begin to brown. Reduce the heat to the lowest setting and continue cooking the onions until they are very brown. The onions are done when they are uniformly brown and very soft and the volume is about one-fifth of the original amount. This will take approximately 1 hour total, but it's worth it.

Increase the heat to medium-high and add the remaining tablespoon butter to the onions. Once the butter has melted, stir in the flour and then cook for 2 minutes. Slowly add 2 cups of the stock and simmer until thickened, approximately 5 minutes (see Note). Add the remaining 4 cups stock and the wine, vinegar, salt, pepper, and thyme. Bring to a simmer, lower the heat, and cook for 5 minutes. Taste for seasoning and add additional salt and pepper as needed.

Garnish the soup by shredding the cheese directly into the soup and topping with a few croutons.

MAKE AHEAD The soup will keep for up to 5 days in the refrigerator; add the cheese and croutons just before serving.

NOTE If your skillet is not wide enough or deep enough to hold 6 cups liquid, transfer the onions to a medium stockpot set over medium-high heat before adding the stock.

TOMATO-CHEDDAR SOUP

MAKES ABOUT 6 CUPS; SERVES 4

AT BEECHER'S, WE SERVE THIS CHUNKY TOMATO SOUP topped with fresh cheese curds and a Breadzel (page 244) on the side. It's like eating a grilled cheese sandwich and tomato soup all in one dish. Rich and creamy and a snap to make, this soup makes a perfect lunch or light dinner.

2 tablespoons unsalted butter
$^1/_2$ medium onion, diced
1 28-ounce can plus 1 14$^1/_2$-ounce can
   crushed tomatoes in puree
$^3/_4$ teaspoon white pepper

$^3/_4$ teaspoon kosher salt
10 ounces semihard cheese (see page 23),
   grated (2$^1/_2$ cups)
$^1/_2$ cup heavy cream

In a large saucepan over medium heat, melt the butter. Add the onion and sauté until soft but not brown, about 4 minutes.

Add the crushed tomatoes, 2$^1/_2$ cups water, pepper, and salt. Bring to a low boil, reduce the heat to low, and simmer, uncovered, for 5 minutes, stirring occasionally.

Add the cheese and cream and stir until the cheese melts, about 2 minutes. Serve hot.

MAKE AHEAD The soup will keep, covered, in the refrigerator for up to 5 days or in the freezer for up to 6 months. Gently reheat over low heat, stirring frequently to avoid burning.

Here is a brief guide to cheese substitutions, arranged by texture. Classifying cheeses by texture is important for cooking because although the flavors can be interchangeable in most recipes, the moisture content varies by type of cheese. In some recipes, a specific cheese is recommended because it's part of a classic combination that cannot be improved upon. We include our favorite brands, but try your local cheeses and experiment.

You'll find we refer to the cheeses by their generic name rather than the traditional names, such as Brie or Parmigiano-Reggiano. This stems from our passion for promoting U.S. cheesemakers, who don't rely on tradition when naming their cheeses, both out of respect for the cheesemakers and because of legal guidelines. American cheesemakers can't call their Parmesan cheese Parmigiano-Reggiano, for example, so we refer to it simply as Parmesan.

Finally, cow's- and sheep's-milk cheeses are the most commonly used cheeses in the book. Although I love the flavor of goat's-milk cheese, it has such a strong, distinctive flavor that it is not an appropriate substitute in most of these dishes.

Fresh Cheese

All cheese starts out as fresh cheese. Fresh cheese is what remains once the whey and curd are separated and the curd is pressed. Soft and smooth in texture, fresh cheese is unprocessed; there is no rind or mold, no heat used, and it is aged only about a week.

- Cream cheese
- Cheese curds
- Mascarpone
- Cottage cheese
- Crème fraîche
- Fromage blanc
- Ricotta

We Recommend
Beecher's Blank Slate (Plain, Honey, and Tapenade)
Bellwether Farms (Fromage Blanc, Crème Fraîche, Ricotta)
Cowgirl Creamery (Clabbered Cottage Cheese, Fromage Blanc, Crème Fraîche)
Sierra Nevada Natural Cream Cheese

Soft Ripened Cheeses

Soft to semisoft in texture, these cheeses are neither pressed nor cooked. They are inoculated with mold spores and ripen from the outside in. This category includes bloomy rind and blue-veined cheeses.

BLOOMY RIND CHEESE

- Camembert
- Brie

We Recommend
Cowgirl Creamery Mt. Tam
Marin French Cheese Co. (a variety of Brie-style cheeses)

BLUE CHEESE

While blue cheese could be categorized as a semi-soft cheese, its distinctive flavor merits a separate category.

We Recommend

Maytag Blue

Point Reyes Original Blue

Rogue Creamery Smokey Blue

Roquefort

Danish Blue

Semisoft Cheeses

These cheeses contain 61 to 69 percent moisture and may or may not be pressed. Firm but moist, many are crumbly in texture. Semisoft cheeses have a smooth, creamy interior with little or no rind, and are sliceable.

- Colby
- Fontina
- Brick
- Havarti
- Monterey Jack
- Mozzarella

We Recommend

Beecher's Just Jack

Mozzarella Company Mozzarella

Vella Jack

Semihard Cheeses

Cooked and pressed, cheeses in this category contain not more than 54 to 63 percent moisture. Semi-hard cheeses are sliceable.

- Cheddar
- Gruyère
- Swiss
- Gouda

- Provolone
- Emmenthaler

We Recommend

Beecher's Flagship

Bellwether Farms San Andreas

Grafton Village Cheddar

Oregon Gourmet Sublimity

Pleasant Valley Smoked Gouda

Hard Cheeses

Hard cheeses are cooked and pressed cheeses that have a moisture content of 49 to 56 percent. They are very firm and can be both sliced and grated.

- Parmesan
- Asiago
- Dry jack
- Romano

We Recommend

Vella Dry Jack and Asiago

Willamette Valley Brindisi Fontina

CRAB AND LEEK CHOWDER

MAKES 4 CUPS; SERVES 2 TO 4

NEW ENGLANDERS HAVE THEIR CLAM CHOWDER; here in the Pacific Northwest we also make chowder with fresh local crab. Even better, this soup can be served cold in the summer and warm in the winter months. Don't let the jalapeño in the recipe scare you; this soup isn't spicy. Seeded, diced, and sautéed, the jalapeño loses most of its heat and adds a nice undertone to the rich crab and creamy potato.

1 tablespoon unsalted butter
1 jalapeño pepper, seeded and diced
2 medium garlic cloves, roughly chopped
1 medium leek, chopped (see Note)
3 cups Crab Stock (page 232) or fish stock
2 medium Yukon Gold potatoes, cut into
 ½-inch cubes
¼ teaspoon kosher salt
¼ teaspoon freshly ground black pepper
Tabasco or other hot sauce, to taste

3 ounces cooked lump crabmeat,
 preferably Dungeness, rinsed and
 drained
¼ cup fresh corn kernels, cut off the cob,
 or frozen, defrosted
¼ cup chopped red bell pepper
Crispy Shallots (recipe follows; optional)
Fresh flat-leaf parsley, chopped, for
 garnish

Melt the butter in a medium saucepan over high heat. Cook until the butter just begins to brown, about 1½ minutes. Add the jalapeño and sauté for 1 minute. Add the garlic and leek and sauté for 1 minute, stirring. Increase the heat to high, add the stock, potatoes, salt, and pepper, and bring to a boil. Reduce the heat to low and let the soup simmer for 15 minutes. Remove the pot from the heat.

Using an immersion blender, puree the soup until smooth. Alternatively, puree the mixture in a food processor or blender. Stir in the hot sauce to taste. Return the pot to low heat and simmer the soup for 15 minutes.

Put the drained crabmeat in a small bowl and pick through it with your hands, removing any pieces of shell.

To serve, divide the chowder among 4 bowls. Garnish each bowl with crabmeat, corn, red bell pepper, and shallot rings. Top with a pinch of parsley.

NOTE Before chopping the leek, cut off the thick green part (about 3 inches of the green end) and slice the leek in half lengthwise. Rinse between the layers to remove dirt.

Crispy Shallots

2 tablespoons all-purpose flour

$\frac{1}{2}$ teaspoon kosher salt

$\frac{1}{4}$ teaspoon freshly ground black pepper

1 shallot, sliced into $\frac{1}{4}$-inch rings

3 tablespoons extra-virgin olive oil

Combine the flour, salt, and pepper in a small bowl. Dredge the shallots in the flour mixture, shaking off any excess flour.

In a medium skillet over high heat, heat the olive oil. Add the shallot rings and cook without stirring until they turn golden brown, about 2 minutes. Turn them over and cook until they are golden and crisp, about 2 minutes. As the shallots finish cooking, remove them to a plate lined with a paper towel.

Gwen Bassetti

With rows of every imaginable type of bread in grocery stores today, it's hard to imagine a time when fresh, artisanal bread wasn't readily available. Artisanal bread—bread that is made by hand without chemical additives, dough enhancers, or artificial ingredients—can now be found in virtually any market around the country. But until Gwen Bassetti opened the doors to the Grand Central Bakery in 1989, there was almost no fresh bread in Seattle. Gwen started in the baking business with a sandwich shop in old Seattle, where she and her partners baked whole-grain breads for their sandwiches. After moving to a farm with her family, Gwen rekindled her passion for baking while visiting San Francisco. There she discovered artisanal breads and brought the techniques back to her home kitchen.

When she opened the Grand Central Bakery, it took one write-up in the local newspaper for crowds to line up around the block. "Without even thinking about it, we were part of a budding food revolution that hit Seattle in the 1990s," she says. Gwen remembers one Christmas when the head baker decided to quell the lines by raising the price

of a loaf by a dollar. "I was shocked, but it didn't stop the customers!"

Gwen attributes her early success to "the novelty of the bread and because we didn't have any competition," but more likely it was her fifteen varieties of Italian artisanal bread that caused the ruckus. "People who had traveled to Europe or people of European heritage loved the bread," says Gwen. "People have a long cultural memory."

The move from small bakery to a large-scale producer of bread didn't happen overnight. "We didn't immediately go into grocery stores because they didn't know how to deal with this kind of bread," she says. "Metropolitan Market was our first customer. You didn't see the rows of fresh bread you see in a Whole Foods today. The display rack my first husband designed is still in the Metropolitan Market." The bakery eventually started selling bread to local restaurants and became a mainstay in local grocery stores. And Seattle was the perfect place to start: "Seattle has always been a pioneer. It's not as provincial as people think. People think of Seattle as this place in a far corner of the country, but it has quite a vibrant food community," she says.

With Gwen's three kids now running the business, the Grand Central Bakery has grown into seven cafés in both Washington State and Oregon, but the commitment to quality is the same. The 4,000 to 6,000 loaves they bake every day in both Seattle and Portland are made from scratch, using local products whenever possible to promote sustainable agriculture. Their flour comes from a mill in Idaho, and they use local fruits and vegetables in their breads, pastries, and café items. Pick up a Como loaf, a Grand Central specialty, on your next trip to the Pacific Northwest.

TOASTED TOMATO-BASIL SANDWICH

MAKES 4 SANDWICHES

THIS IS A SANDWICH THAT REALLY SHOWS OFF THE CHEESE. We use Flagship and Just Jack cheeses, but any semihard cheese, such as Cheddar or Gruyère, will work beautifully. For a heartier sandwich, add a few slices of smoked turkey.

1/4 cup Basic Mayonnaise (page 234) or any all-natural mayonnaise

1 1/2 tablespoons whole-grain mustard

2 dashes Tabasco or other hot sauce

8 slices hearty artisanal white bread

4 ounces semihard cheese (page 23), cut into 8 thin slices

2 tomatoes, sliced 1/4-inch thick

12 fresh basil leaves

2 ounces semisoft cheese (page 23), cut into 8 thin slices

In a small bowl, whisk together the mayonnaise, mustard, and Tabasco sauce until fully combined.

To assemble the sandwiches, spread half of the mayonnaise mixture on 4 slices of bread. Layer 2 slices semihard cheese, 2 slices tomato, 3 basil leaves, and 2 slices semisoft cheese on top of each piece of bread. Spread the remaining 4 slices bread and place them, mayonnaise side down, on top of the cheese slices.

Heat a large skillet over medium heat and put the sandwiches in the pan. Cook until the cheese has melted and the bread is golden brown, about 3 minutes per side. Serve warm.

MAKE AHEAD The spread will keep in an airtight container in the refrigerator for up to 3 days. (If you are using store-bought mayonnaise, the spread can be stored for up to 1 month.)

TOASTED BRIE AND SWEET THAI CHILI SAUCE SANDWICH

MAKES 4 SANDWICHES

GOOEY, OOZING CHEESE IS ALWAYS A HIT, especially when it's sandwiched between two slices of crisp toasted bread. The contrast of rich Brie and the sweet and spicy chili sauce in this combination is sublime. Leave the rind on the Brie; it's a natural, edible part of the cheese.

8 ounces Brie-style cheese, cut into 8 slices

8 slices hearty artisanal white bread

4 tablespoons Sweet Thai Chili Sauce (recipe follows)

Lay 2 slices of cheese on each of 4 slices of the bread. Spread 1 tablespoon chili sauce on each of the remaining 4 slices bread and lay them, sauce side down, on top of the cheese.

Heat a large skillet over medium heat and put the sandwiches in the pan. Cook until the cheese has melted and the bread is golden brown, about 3 minutes per side. Serve warm.

Sweet Thai Chili Sauce

MAKES 1 CUP

This sweet and savory sandwich spread or dipping sauce is a natural pairing for cheese.

4 garlic cloves, peeled

1/4 teaspoon kosher salt

1 1/2 teaspoons red pepper flakes

1/2 cup cider vinegar

2/3 cup gently packed light brown sugar

Using a mortar and pestle, pound or mash the garlic and salt together. Stir in the pepper flakes and set aside.

Place the vinegar in a small, nonreactive saucepan (see Note). Bring it to a boil over high heat. Stir in the sugar, reduce the heat, and simmer for 5 minutes. Stir in the garlic mixture and cook for 1 minute. Remove the pan from the heat. Let the sauce cool to room temperature before using.

MAKE AHEAD The sauce will keep in a glass or ceramic container for 5 days in the refrigerator.

NOTE A nonreactive saucepan refers to one made of metals, such as stainless steel, that have no negative reaction to foods that are cooked in them. Reactive metals, like copper, aluminum, and cast iron, react detrimentally with certain foods, particularly those that are acidic, such as lemon, tomatoes, and vinegar, imparting an off flavor and sometimes color.

TOASTED PROSCIUTTO, CHEDDAR, AND APPLE SANDWICH

MAKES 4 SANDWICHES

CHEDDAR CHEESE AND APPLES are a classic American pairing, and a little prosciutto elevates a simple grilled cheese sandwich to a satisfying midday meal. In this sandwich we use nitrate-free prosciutto, which is available in most specialty stores.

8 teaspoons whole-grain mustard

4 teaspoons honey

8 ounces aged Cheddar, cut into 8 thin slices

8 slices hearty artisanal white bread

4 thin slices prosciutto (about 2 ounces)

1/2 Fuji apple or other sweet apple, cut into 8 thin slices

Freshly ground black pepper (optional)

In a small bowl, combine the mustard and honey. Set aside.

To assemble the sandwiches, lay 1 slice of cheese on each of 4 slices of the bread. On top of each cheese slice, layer 1 slice prosciutto, 2 slices apple, and 1 more slice cheese. Grind pepper on top of the cheese, if desired.

Spread 1 tablespoon of the honey mustard on each of the remaining 4 slices of bread and lay them, honey-mustard side down, on top of the cheese slices.

Heat a large skillet over medium heat and put the sandwiches in the pan. Cook until the cheese has melted and the bread is golden brown, about 3 minutes per side. Serve warm.

apples

It's hard to keep up with apples. Once you think you know them all, a new variety appears in the grocery store. Cameo®, Cripps Pink, Jonathan, and Rome Beauty—everyone has an opinion about which variety is the best, especially in Washington State. Less well known, but just as delicious, are the Ben Davis and the spicy Jonathan apples from Idaho. Each has its own personality: Cripps Pink begs to be sliced and eaten plain, but sweetens any apple dessert; Jonagolds make a sweet-tart applesauce; and the spicy sweet Braeburn complements a piece of cheese or makes a divine apple pie. It used to be a Red Delicious apple world, but recently farmers have been bringing back the heirloom varieties.

Drive east from Seattle and you'll see 225,000 acres of orchards tucked in the eastern foothills of the towering, snowcapped Cascade Mountains. With elevations of 500 to 3,000 feet above sea level, the landscape allows farmers to irrigate the orchards with mountain water. Visit in late April and you'll be transfixed by the beautiful white apple blossoms; early fall brings the first sign of fruit. Organic apples thrive here; the climate and temperatures reduce the chance of disease, which in turn eliminates the need for pesticides. Washington is the leading organic apple producer in the country. More than 25 percent of the state's shippers are certified organic, producing 2 to 3 million boxes of apples a year.

The dwarf variety is the most commonly planted apple tree, so the 35,000 to 40,000 pickers who come to the region every fall can easily climb ladders to the top of the trees and pick the fruit by hand. (Because there is no machine that can pick apples, all 10 to 12 billion apples that come from Washington State each year are hand-picked.)

Mounds of apples fill produce aisles year-round, but they taste best after the fall harvest, between September and November. (No wonder the teacher always gets an apple.) They keep best in a cool, dark place, although they will last a few days in the refrigerator.

CORNMEAL-CRUSTED OYSTER SANDWICH

MAKES 4 TO 6 SANDWICHES

WHETHER YOU FRY THEM, SAUTÉ THEM, OR EAT THEM RAW, fresh oysters are simply sublime. Our local favorites are the tiny Olympia oyster (the only oyster native to the Pacific Northwest), plump Pacific oysters, European Flat oysters, and petite Kumamotos. The large Pacific oysters are the best for frying. Coated in cornmeal, they make a savory sandwich, but fried oysters also make an impressive appetizer. One tip: Use two hands while battering the oysters—one hand to dip in the flour and one to dunk in the egg and cornmeal—so you don't end up with two messy hands.

1½ to 2 dozen extra-small fresh oysters or
    2 10-ounce jars oysters (about
    5 oysters per sandwich)
¼ cup all-purpose flour
2 large eggs
5 tablespoons cornmeal, or as needed
1¼ teaspoons kosher salt
¾ teaspoon freshly ground black pepper

1 teaspoon Old Bay Seasoning
1 tablespoon unsalted butter
1 tablespoon extra-virgin olive oil
8 slices hearty artisanal white bread
4 tablespoons Southwest Mayonnaise
  (page 235)
6 leaves romaine lettuce, chopped

If using fresh oysters, shuck them. Drain jarred oysters thoroughly in a strainer and set aside.

In three separate bowls, place the flour, eggs, and 2 tablespoons of the cornmeal. Add ¼ teaspoon of the salt and ¼ teaspoon of the pepper to the eggs and beat well. Stir the Old Bay, remaining teaspoon salt, and remaining ½ teaspoon pepper into the flour.

Heat a medium skillet over medium-high heat. Add the butter and olive oil and stir until the butter has melted.

Dip 1 oyster first in the flour, then the eggs, and then the cornmeal, coating it evenly. (The cornmeal may begin to clump as you bread the oysters. About every five oysters, add 1 more tablespoon of cornmeal to the cornmeal bowl, or, if necessary, scoop the clumped cornmeal out of the bowl or start a fresh bowl of cornmeal.)

Add the oysters to the skillet and cook them for 1 minute on each side, or until the crust turns golden brown. Transfer the oysters to a plate lined with paper towels.

To assemble the sandwiches, spread ½ tablespoon of the mayonnaise on each slice of bread. Layer 5 oysters and some lettuce on top of 4 slices. Place the remaining 4 slices bread on top of the lettuce. Serve immediately.

Paul Shipman

While there are hundreds of microbreweries around the United States today, twenty years ago beer options were often limited to canned beer or home brewing. Paul Shipman, cofounder and chief executive officer of Redhook Ale Brewery in Woodinville, Washington, brought craft beer to the forefront of the beverage industry and helped turn the Pacific Northwest into the hotbed of microbrews in the world today.

Paul started in the beverage business working in the finance department at Château Ste. Michelle Winery in Eastern Washington. After the winery passed on an idea to create a champagne division, Paul jumped at the chance to create his own company. In 1981, at a meeting with investor and cofounder Gordon Bowker, Paul was told one thing that changed his life: that he should drop the champagne idea and open a microbrewery instead. At the time, the beer industry was dominated by big players such as Miller and Coors Light, with no local breweries making handcrafted beer. Redhook Brewery was born in an old transmission shop, but success was far from overnight. As Paul describes it, "Our venture had a lot of kinks. The beer wasn't that great. It took us two years to get it right." With his knowledge of fine wine, Paul didn't expect that making a great beer would be such a challenge. "I underestimated what it would take to make a fine beer. I knew fine wine, but in reality, the beermaker is up against a more difficult set of hurdles than the winemaker," says Paul. "The reason is the winemaker starts with the grapes from the vineyard and is halfway there. The beermaker has no advantage—he has to make the beer from scratch."

While Redhook was finding its footing, Paul found support from the Pacific Northwest community. "When I think about how difficult it was to start and what we were up against, I think of the incredibly supportive environment in Seattle and the Northwest," says Paul. "Even though we were struggling, the bars, the newspapers, and the bank all felt it was a matter of civic pride for the brewery to succeed. Coming from the East Coast, it was incredibly heartening to feel the support," he says. "There is something magical about this place. . . . There's another dimension that is missing in most places, and that is the general support for the tastemaking entrepreneur. I saw it crystal clear coming in as an outsider."

After a scientist, or "beer wizard," as Paul describes him, appeared on the brewery's doorstep in 1984 and talked to him about changing his recipe for Ballard Bitter, his trademark beer, Redhook IPA, was created. That was the beginning of Redhook's success. Today Redhook operates two breweries, one in Woodinville and one in Portsmouth, New Hampshire, and makes nine different beers, including seasonal brews, for distribution in forty-eight states.

SALADS

MEDITERRANEAN SALAD

JEWELED CABBAGE SLAW

FRESH TOMATO AND CHEESE CURD SALAD

GOLDEN BEET SALAD

BLACK-EYED PEA AND MUSTARD GREEN SALAD

EASIEST CRAB SALAD

ICEBERG WEDGE WITH BLUE CHEESE–LEMON VINAIGRETTE

CHICKEN-AVOCADO SALAD

CHICKEN SALAD WITH CORN AND CILANTRO

CRUNCHY CHICKEN AND RICE SALAD

BENNETT'S COBB SALAD

NORTHWEST NIÇOISE

PENNE AND SMOKED MOZZARELLA SALAD

POLKA DOT PASTA SALAD

MEDITERRANEAN SALAD

SERVES 4 TO 6

THE TENDER FLAVOR OF BUTTER LETTUCE, often called Boston or bibb lettuce, is celebrated in this simple salad. We find locally grown butter lettuce from May through October, but it's also available year-round from slightly farther afield. Herbs, oranges, and olives complete this light and luscious salad.

4 sweet oranges, such as Caracara
1 teaspoon sugar
2 heads butter lettuce, core removed,
    leaves torn into bite-size pieces
1/4 cup chopped pitted green olives
2 plum tomatoes, chopped
2 green onions (white and green parts),
    chopped

1 cup Herbed Croutons (page 243) or
    store-bought croutons
2 tablespoons roughly chopped fresh basil
2 teaspoons roughly chopped fresh mint
Lemon Vinaigrette (recipe follows)
2 ounces hard cheese (page 23), thinly
    shaved, for garnish (1/2 cup)
Freshly ground black pepper, to taste

Peel the oranges and separate them into segments. Mix the orange segments with the sugar in a large bowl and let sit for 5 minutes.

Combine the orange segments, lettuce, olives, tomatoes, green onions, croutons, basil, mint, and vinaigrette.

Divide the lettuce mixture evenly among chilled salad plates. Top each with cheese and freshly ground pepper to taste.

Lemon Vinaigrette

MAKES ABOUT ²/₃ CUP

This is a great all-purpose vinaigrette that can dress a salad as easily as it can be poured on grilled vegetables or served as a dipping sauce for bread.

¹/₃ cup freshly squeezed lemon juice (1 to 2 lemons)

1 tablespoon minced garlic (about 3 cloves)

2 teaspoons kosher salt

1 teaspoon freshly ground black pepper

¹/₄ teaspoon dried basil

¹/₄ teaspoon dried oregano

¹/₃ cup extra-virgin olive oil

In a medium bowl, whisk together the lemon juice, garlic, salt, pepper, basil, oregano, and olive oil. Taste for seasoning and add more salt and pepper, as needed.

MAKE AHEAD The vinaigrette will keep for up to 3 days in the refrigerator.

tomatoes

There are three basic categories of tomato: bite-size, plum, and slicing tomatoes. Bite-size varieties include cherry tomatoes and pear tomatoes (red or yellow). Plum tomatoes are also known as Italian or Roma tomatoes, and they are fairly small and shaped like an egg. These are meatier and less juicy than slicing tomatoes, so they're ideal for sauces. Slicing tomatoes include beefsteak and globe tomatoes.

Heirloom tomatoes are nonhybrid (open-pollinated) varieties that have existed for at least fifty years. Small producers have started planting these tomato varietals, which come in a wide variety of shapes, colors, and flavors. Some well-known heirloom varieties include Brandywine, Hawaiian Pineapple, and Green Zebra. Full of flavor, heirlooms are available at farmer's markets and gourmet grocery stores during tomato season. Commercial farmers stay away from heirloom varieties because they're more difficult to grow and produce lower yields. Also, because they have thin skins and a short life, heirlooms can't be packed and shipped like the heartier varieties.

Depending on locale, tomato season usually runs June through October. This is when tomatoes deserve to be eaten. Although the cool Pacific Northwest climate isn't ideal for growing them commercially, the tomatoes that are grown in our short season—mostly by small farmers and in backyards—are like no other. If you see a tomato in your grocery store in February, chances are it came from Mexico, Canada, or California. Those tomatoes are usually picked green in the field and ripened with ethylene gas or in special warming rooms, and they don't have the texture, aroma, or flavor of vine-ripened fruit. Hothouse tomatoes are another common type of tomato. Grown in greenhouses, hothouse tomatoes were largely developed by the Canadians, who have a very short growing season. Canada now leads the export market for the hothouse variety.

Tomatoes purchased from a farmstand or farmer's market are by far superior in flavor and texture, but grocery stores are starting to stock more varieties. Out-of-season tomatoes not only lack flavor, they're not as healthy, either. Lycopene, the cancer-fighting plant compound found in tomato skins that gives them their red color, is significantly diminished in a winter tomato. If you want to make a dish with tomatoes outside of tomato season and can't find good ones, high-quality canned tomatoes are the best substitute in cooked dishes.

Buy tomatoes that are free of bruises or blemishes (cracks at the stem end are fine, though). Ripe tomatoes should smell fragrant and feel soft and yielding to the touch. Size won't indicate flavor or quality. A quick size guide: large tomatoes weigh about 8 ounces, and three to four medium tomatoes equal 1 pound. Skip tomatoes that are stored in refrigerated bins; the cold damages them.

Store tomatoes at room temperature (above 55°F.), out of direct sunlight. You can ripen tomatoes by placing them in a paper bag with an apple. Ripe tomatoes will keep for a day or two at room temperature.

JEWELED CABBAGE SLAW

SERVES 4 TO 6

JÍCAMA IS A ROOT VEGETABLE that is used throughout Latin America. It looks like a large radish and has a clean, neutral flavor that adds a crisp texture to any dish. This refreshing salad, with its Asian vinaigrette, will be a welcome addition to a summer picnic or barbecue. I leave out the salt and pepper because the soy sauce provides the seasoning.

3 tablespoons soy sauce

3 tablespoons rice vinegar

3 tablespoons neutral-flavored cooking oil, such as canola or soybean

$1/2$ teaspoon sesame oil

1 tablespoon plus 2 teaspoons sugar

$1/4$ teaspoon red pepper flakes

$1/2$ head green cabbage, cored and thinly sliced (8 cups)

1 small carrot, thinly sliced

$1/2$ red bell pepper, sliced

$1/2$ medium jícama, thinly sliced

3 green onions (white and green parts), thinly sliced

Toasted slivered almonds, for garnish

To make the dressing, in a large bowl, whisk together the soy sauce, vinegar, cooking oil, sesame oil, sugar, and red pepper flakes.

Add the cabbage, carrot, bell pepper, jícama, and green onions, and toss the vegetables with the dressing. Garnish with the toasted almonds and serve immediately.

MAKE AHEAD Refrigerate the dressing and the vegetables separately for up to 1 day; toss together just before serving.

FRESH TOMATO AND CHEESE CURD SALAD

SERVES 6

THIS SALAD SHOWS OFF PERFECTLY RIPE TOMATOES and creamy cheese curds. Cheese curds are a type of fresh cheese that remains when the whey is drained. The curds are compressed, cut into loaves, and then milled into larger curds. The reduced tomato liquid adds to the salad's savory flavor without creating excess liquid in the bowl, preventing the salad from getting soggy. Skip this recipe if tomatoes aren't in season; only the ripest summer tomatoes will do.

5 large tomatoes, preferably heirloom, chopped
1 teaspoon kosher salt
4 ounces Herbed Croutons (page 243) or store-bought croutons (about 2 cups)
1 tablespoon minced fresh cilantro
1 tablespoon thinly sliced fresh chives

1 avocado, sliced
8 ounces fresh cheese curds or fresh mozzarella, cut into $1/4$-inch pieces (2 cups)
3 tablespoons extra-virgin olive oil
1 tablespoon white wine vinegar
Freshly ground black pepper, to taste

Place the tomatoes in a large bowl. Add the salt, toss, and let rest for 5 minutes.

Drain the tomato liquid from the tomatoes into a small, nonreactive saucepan (see Note, page 28). Cook the liquid slowly over medium heat until reduced by half, about 15 minutes. Set the liquid aside in a small bowl to cool to room temperature.

Add the croutons, reduced tomato liquid, cilantro, chives, avocado, cheese curds, olive oil, vinegar, and black pepper to the tomatoes and gently toss. Let stand for 3 minutes and then toss again.

Serve at room temperature.

MAKE AHEAD The salad will keep, covered, for up to 2 days in the refrigerator; add the avocado just before serving.

GOLDEN BEET SALAD

SERVES 4 TO 6

SALADS NEED NOT FOCUS ON THE LETTUCE. Here the greens take a back seat to vibrant golden beets. The salty, creamy blue cheese and the crunchy walnuts complement the sweet beets. Roasting the beets in water prevents them from drying out.

1¼ pounds golden beets, trimmed and rinsed

1½ tablespoons rice vinegar

½ teaspoon kosher salt

¼ teaspoon freshly ground black pepper

1 tablespoon extra-virgin olive oil

¼ teaspoon whole-grain or Dijon mustard

1 ounce spinach leaves or baby spinach, sliced (about 1 cup)

3 tablespoons toasted walnuts (page 195)

1 ounce blue cheese, crumbled (¼ cup)

Preheat the oven to 400°F.

Place the beets in a roasting pan and add water to a depth of ½ inch. Cover the pan with foil and bake until the beets are easily pierced with a fork, about 1½ hours. Set the beets aside until they are cool enough to handle. Peel and rinse off any pieces of skin. Slice the beets into ½-inch-thick rounds, and then cut them into ¼-inch-thick sticks. Let the beets cool to room temperature.

Toss the beets with the rice vinegar, salt, and pepper. Add the olive oil and mustard and toss with the spinach. Garnish with the toasted walnuts and crumbled blue cheese.

MAKE AHEAD You can roast the beets up to 3 days in advance; toss them just before serving.

BLACK-EYED PEA AND MUSTARD GREEN SALAD

SERVES 4 TO 6

THIS IS A PASTA & CO RECIPE that's been a customer favorite for years. Inspired by the classic Southern ingredient black-eyed peas, this healthy salad has the sharp flavor of mustard greens, while fresh tarragon adds an extra zing. For a heartier salad, add a few slices of leftover grilled, roasted, or poached chicken.

$1^{1}/_{2}$ cups dried black-eyed peas, rinsed and picked over, or 2 15-ounce cans, drained and rinsed

$2^{3}/_{4}$ teaspoons kosher salt

2 tablespoons minced fresh tarragon, or 2 teaspoons dried

2 teaspoons ground fennel seed

$1/_{4}$ cup sherry wine vinegar

$1^{1}/_{2}$ tablespoons whole-grain mustard

$1^{1}/_{2}$ teaspoons honey

$1/_{4}$ teaspoon red pepper flakes

$1/_{4}$ teaspoon freshly ground black pepper

$3/_{4}$ cup plus 2 tablespoons extra-virgin olive oil

$1/_{4}$ cup chopped fresh tarragon

1 bunch mustard greens (leaves only), sliced

1 bunch green onions (white and green parts), thinly sliced

12 ounces semihard cheese (page 23), grated (3 cups)

If using dried peas, put them in a medium saucepan and add enough cold water to cover by 2 inches. Bring the peas to a boil over medium-high heat and cook for 25 to 30 minutes, or until they are tender but not too soft. Add 2 teaspoons of the salt, and continue to cook for 5 minutes. Drain well. While the peas are cooking, prepare the dressing. Whisk the 2 tablespoons tarragon, fennel, vinegar, mustard, honey, $3/_{4}$ teaspoon salt, red pepper flakes, black pepper, and olive oil together in a large bowl.

Combine the cooked or canned peas with the dressing. Refrigerate for 30 minutes.

Add the $1/_{4}$ cup tarragon, mustard greens, and green onions to the peas, and toss to combine. Top with the cheese. Serve chilled or at room temperature.

MAKE AHEAD You can prepare this salad up to 2 days in advance, but add the greens no more than 1 hour before serving. Otherwise, the greens will wilt.

EASIEST CRAB SALAD

THIS LIGHT SALAD WILL BECOME A GO-TO RECIPE in your kitchen. Taking only minutes to prepare, it can be served as a first course or as a main course for a summer lunch. Or spoon the salad on slices of fresh bread for a seafood sandwich. We prefer Dungeness crab, but King or blue crab can be substituted. Or skip the crab and use prawns, bay shrimp, or lobster instead. Add just a sprinkling of celery seed; its flavor is very strong, and you will need only a very small amount.

12 ounces cooked lump crabmeat, preferably Dungeness crab, rinsed and drained (about 2 cups)

2 green onions (white and green parts), thinly sliced

1/4 red bell pepper, diced

1/2 stalk celery, diced

2 tablespoons extra-virgin olive oil

1/4 teaspoon grated lemon zest

1 tablespoon freshly squeezed lemon juice

1 1/2 teaspoons grated fresh horseradish or store-bought creamy prepared horseradish

1/4 teaspoon Tabasco or other hot sauce

1 tablespoon chopped fresh dill

2 tablespoons chopped fresh basil

Pinch of celery seed

1/4 teaspoon Old Bay Seasoning

Put the crabmeat in a large bowl and pick through it with your hands, removing any pieces of shell. Add the green onions, bell pepper, celery, olive oil, lemon zest, lemon juice, horseradish, hot sauce, dill, basil, celery seed, and Old Bay. Refrigerate until ready to serve.

MAKE AHEAD The crab salad can be stored in the refrigerator for up to 2 days, covered.

ICEBERG WEDGE
with Blue Cheese–Lemon Vinaigrette

SERVES 6

TRADITIONAL ICEBERG WEDGE SALADS arrive smothered in heavy blue cheese dressing. Our version has a lighter dressing, thanks to rice vinegar and lemon, but still maintains that tangy blue cheese flavor.

1 head iceberg lettuce, core removed
Blue Cheese–Lemon Vinaigrette (recipe
    follows)
1 large tomato, diced
2 ounces hazelnuts (about 1/2 cup), lightly
    toasted (page 195) and roughly chopped

6 ounces blue cheese, crumbled
    (1 1/4 cups)
Freshly ground black pepper, to taste

Cut the head of lettuce in half by slicing it from the top to the bottom. Cut each half into 3 wedges.

Drizzle 2 to 3 tablespoons of dressing over each wedge, and then layer the tomato, hazelnuts, blue cheese, and pepper on top. Serve cold.

Blue Cheese–Lemon Vinaigrette

MAKES ABOUT 1 CUP

2 tablespoons freshly squeezed lemon
    juice
2 tablespoons rice vinegar
1/2 cup extra-virgin olive oil

2 1/2 ounces blue cheese, crumbled (about
    1/2 cup)
1/4 teaspoon kosher salt
1/4 teaspoon freshly ground black pepper

In a small bowl, whisk together the lemon juice, rice vinegar, and olive oil. Add the blue cheese and mash it with the whisk to break it up. Season the dressing with the salt and pepper and whisk to emulsify. The blue cheese should be well blended into the dressing.

MAKE AHEAD The dressing will keep, covered, in the refrigerator for up to 5 days.

CHICKEN-AVOCADO SALAD

SERVES 4

CHICKEN AND AVOCADO SHARE THE SPOTLIGHT in this simple yet elegant salad. This will become an instant favorite of the avocado lovers in your house, and it's an easy lunch or quick dinner.

½ cup freshly squeezed grapefruit juice (about ½ grapefruit)

1 tablespoon freshly squeezed lime juice

1 tablespoon diced shallot

½ teaspoon chili powder

1 teaspoon whole-grain mustard

1 Fresno chile pepper or any hot red chile pepper, seeded and finely chopped

1 tablespoon chopped fresh chives

½ cup extra-virgin olive oil

Kosher salt and freshly ground black pepper

2 cups cubed cooked chicken (page 230; about 2 chicken breast halves)

2 tablespoons Basic Mayonnaise (page 234) or any store-bought mayonnaise

2 avocados, sliced lengthwise

To make the dressing, in a small bowl, combine the grapefruit juice, lime juice, shallot, chili powder, mustard, chiles, chives, olive oil, 1 teaspoon salt, and ¼ teaspoon black pepper. Stir until well combined and set aside.

Put the chicken in a large bowl. Add the mayonnaise, 1 teaspoon salt, and ¼ teaspoon black pepper. Add 1 tablespoon of the dressing and stir until well combined. Taste for seasoning and add salt and black pepper, as needed.

To serve, fan one-quarter of the avocado slices on the bottom of each of 4 plates. Sprinkle with salt and black pepper. Divide the chicken on top of the avocado and spoon dressing over everything.

MAKE AHEAD The chicken salad will keep for 3 days refrigerated. Do not cut the avocado until just before serving. The dressing can be made up to 3 days ahead.

CHICKEN SALAD
with Corn and Cilantro

SERVES 4

LEFTOVER POACHED CHICKEN FROM OUR CHICKEN STOCK RECIPE has seemingly endless creative uses. Serve the salad over fresh greens, or roll the chicken in a wrap for a quick lunch. Fresh corn and bell peppers add both flavor and crunch to this dish.

1/2 cup extra-virgin olive oil

1/2 cup rice vinegar

1/4 cup freshly squeezed lime juice (1 to 2 limes)

2 teaspoons chili powder

2 teaspoons ground cumin

1/2 teaspoon garlic powder

2 teaspoons kosher salt

1 teaspoon freshly ground black pepper

1/2 teaspoon Tabasco or other hot sauce

4 cups cubed poached chicken (page 230)

2 large ears yellow corn, kernels removed (about 1 1/3 cups)

1/2 cup chopped fresh cilantro

1/2 red bell pepper, diced

4 green onions (white and green parts), thinly sliced

2 jalapeño peppers, seeded and diced

To make the dressing, whisk together the olive oil, vinegar, lime juice, chili powder, cumin, garlic powder, salt, black pepper, and hot sauce in medium bowl.

Add the chicken, corn, cilantro, bell pepper, green onions, and jalapeños, and stir well to coat. Serve cold or at room temperature.

MAKE AHEAD The salad will keep, covered, for up to 1 day in the refrigerator.

chicken

Finding a chicken that actually tastes like chicken is a challenge with today's poultry methods. Often the pure flavor of chicken is masked by commercial farming techniques that prize size and speedy growth over flavor. There are big differences in flavor, price, and health benefits between processed chickens and chickens from small producers. Here's an explanation of commonly used terms to help you choose chickens.

There are three categories of raw chicken: organic, free-range, and conventional. Organic chickens consume feed, starting in their second day of life, that has been grown without chemical fertilizers, pesticides, fungicides, herbicides, or genetically modified grains, and are fed no animal or poultry byproducts. They are never kept in cages; are never given hormones or antibiotics; have adequate housing with access to the outside and sunlight, ventilation, fresh water, and a clean, dry bed; and are frequently inspected by regulating agencies. These procedures ensure the chickens' health by reducing their stress and thereby reducing illness and the need for antibiotics. It takes twelve weeks to produce an organic chicken.

Free-range chickens lie somewhere in the middle between organic and conventional chickens. Free-range chickens are defined by the U.S. Department of Agriculture (USDA) as "animals whose producers have demonstrated that the animals have been allowed access to the outside." There are no requirements about how much access or how many minutes per day. They do not have to be fed organic feed. Free-range does not necessarily mean organic.

Conventional chickens are ready to be processed in about six weeks. Often housed with thousands of other chickens and fed in artificial light for up to twenty hours a day, they are given antibiotics and drugs to speed their growth, fatten them more quickly, and keep them disease-free.

Unlike *organic,* the term *all-natural* is not a USDA-regulated term and therefore can mean just about anything. Many companies may claim their all-natural chicken is free of antibiotics and other chemicals. The goal is to lead the consumer to believe that *all-natural* is as good as *organic,* but short of a laboratory test, there is no way to be sure. *USDA Organic* on the label means the product meets the requirements of, and is certified by, the National Organic Standards Board (NOSB).

If you can, go online and research who is behind the supplier before making a decision. Buying chickens from a local purveyor at a farmer's market where you can talk to the farmer directly is ideal, but remember that pasture-raised chickens get more exercise and have stronger (which translates to tougher) muscles. But they are also more flavorful and have high amounts of vitamin E, omega-3 fatty acids, and less total fat. If you don't have access to a farmer's market, look for organic chickens in your local supermarket, or talk to your butcher about the chickens he or she carries.

CRUNCHY CHICKEN AND RICE SALAD

SERVES 6

THIS HEALTHY SALAD, made with crunchy cabbage, sweet carrot, juicy chicken, and fresh cilantro, gets a bite from the lime jalapeño dressing.

1½ cups brown rice

2½ cups shredded or cubed cooked chicken (page 230; about 2 large breast halves)

3 green onions (white and green parts), thinly sliced

½ head green cabbage, cored and thinly sliced (8 cups)

¼ cup chopped fresh cilantro

Lime Jalapeño Dressing (recipe follows)

1 small carrot, thinly sliced

Cook the rice according to package instructions. Transfer the cooked rice to a large bowl and let it cool to room temperature.

Add the chicken, about three-quarters of the green onions, the cabbage, and the cilantro to the rice. Pour the dressing over the mixture and toss until well coated. Garnish with the carrots and the remaining green onions.

MAKE AHEAD The salad will keep, covered, in the refrigerator for up to 1 day.

Lime Jalapeño Dressing

MAKES 1¼ CUPS

The secret ingredient of this tangy, spicy dressing is fish sauce, or "nam pla." Made from small, dried fish, nam pla is a staple in Southeast Asian cooking; its strong, distinctive flavor is mellowed by the lime. Adjust the level of spiciness by adding jalapeños or leaving them out entirely.

¼ cup rice vinegar

⅓ cup fish sauce (nam pla)

½ cup freshly squeezed lime juice (about 3 limes)

2 tablespoons minced garlic (about 6 cloves)

4 jalapeño peppers, seeded and minced

¼ cup sugar

½ teaspoon red pepper flakes

In a small bowl, whisk together the vinegar, fish sauce, lime juice, 1 tablespoon water, garlic, jalapeños, sugar, and red pepper flakes until the sugar has dissolved.

MAKE AHEAD The dressing will keep, covered, in the refrigerator for up to 7 days.

BENNETT'S COBB SALAD

SERVES 4

COBB SALAD IS A LUNCHTIME STAPLE, and when a few new ingredients such as crab, crispy prosciutto, and lime-jalapeño dressing are thrown in the mix, the classic just gets better. The Curried Crab Lumps can be made one day in advance and kept in the refrigerator.

2 ounces (about 4 slices) thinly sliced prosciutto, chopped

1 large tomato, diced

1/4 teaspoon kosher salt

2 romaine lettuce hearts

3/4 cup Lime Jalapeño Dressing (page 53)

10 ounces cooked lump crabmeat, preferably Dungeness, rinsed and drained (about 2 cups)

1 large avocado, sliced lengthwise

4 ounces semihard cheese (page 23), grated (1 cup)

Curried Crab Lumps (recipe follows)

Sea salt and freshly ground black pepper

In a small skillet over high heat, sauté the prosciutto for 5 minutes until crispy. Remove from the heat and set aside.

Place the tomatoes in a small bowl and mix in the kosher salt. Set aside.

To serve, place half a romaine heart on each of 4 plates. Gently separate the leaves, fanning them out so the green ends are spread across the top of the plate, with the harder ends still together at the bottom. Drizzle each serving with 2 tablespoons of the dressing.

Arrange the crabmeat, avocado slices, tomatoes, and cheese in individual mounds across the lettuce.

Drizzle 1 tablespoon dressing over each salad, then sprinkle with the crisp prosciutto. In the center of the salad, place 1 crab lump. Finally, sprinkle with sea salt and freshly ground pepper.

Curried Crab Lumps

1 ounce cooked lump crabmeat, rinsed and drained

1 tablespoon unsalted butter

1 tablespoon capers, drained

1 tablespoon diced shallot

1 teaspoon sweet curry powder

Put the crabmeat in a bowl and pick through it, removing any pieces of shell.

In a small skillet over medium heat, melt the butter. Add the capers and sauté them for 1 minute. Add the shallots, stir, and remove from the heat. Stir in the curry powder. Gently fold in the crabmeat until it is covered with the sauce.

MAKE AHEAD Make the crab lumps up to 1 day ahead and refrigerate.

NORTHWEST NIÇOISE

SERVES 6

THIS IS A GREEN-FREE SALAD where vegetables take center stage. The olive dressing makes this dish stand out, with fennel adding an extra crunch. Use as little or as much tuna as you wish; we prefer it as a background note.

DRESSING

3 small jarred piquillo peppers or 3 small
    jarred roasted red peppers, drained
1 tablespoon chopped fresh chives
6 pitted kalamata olives
1 garlic clove, peeled
6 tablespoons extra-virgin olive oil
3 tablespoons rice vinegar
1/4 teaspoon kosher salt
1/4 teaspoon freshly ground black pepper

SALAD

1 fennel bulb
1 tablespoon extra-virgin olive oil
Kosher salt and freshly ground black
    pepper
4 medium red potatoes (about 2 pounds)
2 tablespoons unsalted butter
12 ounces green beans
10 cherry tomatoes, halved
1 or 2 6-ounce cans chunk tuna, drained
12 kalamata olives, pitted and chopped,
    for garnish

To make the dressing, using a food processor or blender, puree the piquillo peppers, chives, olives, garlic, olive oil, rice vinegar, salt, and black pepper.

Reserve the feathery tops of the fennel and slice the bulb in half. Cut out the core, and then thinly slice the fennel. Heat a large skillet over medium-high heat. Add the olive oil and fennel and season with salt and pepper. Cook for 3 to 4 minutes, stirring occasionally, until the fennel begins to turn translucent. Remove it to a large serving bowl.

While the fennel is cooking, slice the potatoes in half lengthwise, and then slice them again crosswise into 1/2-inch-thick half-moons.

Wipe out the skillet with a paper towel, return it to high heat, and melt the butter in it. Add the potatoes and season with salt and pepper. Cook the potatoes for 2 minutes, or until they begin to brown. Reduce the heat to medium, flip the potatoes, and cook for an additional 10 to 15 minutes, stirring occasionally, until they are golden brown and tender. Remove the potatoes to the bowl with the fennel. Allow to cool to room temperature.

While the vegetables cool, blanch the green beans for 2 minutes in a pot of salted boiling water and rinse with cold water to cool. Drain well. Add the green beans, cherry tomatoes, and tuna to the bowl with the fennel and potatoes. Add two-thirds of the dressing to the salad and toss.

To serve, garnish with the olives, remaining dressing, and reserved fennel tops.

MAKE AHEAD The dressing can be made up to
3 days ahead.

PENNE AND
SMOKED MOZZARELLA SALAD

SERVES 6

WHILE FRESH MOZZARELLA IS USED IN AN ENDLESS VARIETY of pastas, pizzas, and salads, smoked mozzarella adds more flavor. It is made by smoking cheese over wood to produce a smoky, creamy result. This easy pasta salad makes a standout lunch dish, with the mayonnaise lending extra creaminess. You can adjust the amount of dressing according to taste.

8 ounces penne (about 3¼ cups)
1 cup Basic Mayonnaise (page 234) or any
    all-natural mayonnaise
¼ cup extra-virgin olive oil
½ cup rice vinegar
2 ounces Parmesan or other hard cheese
    (page 23), shredded (½ cup)
1 large garlic clove, minced
1½ teaspoons freshly ground black
    pepper

½ teaspoon kosher salt
¼ teaspoon Tabasco or other hot sauce
Pinch of ground cloves
1 jarred roasted red bell pepper, drained
    and diced (½ cup)
8 ounces smoked mozzarella, diced
    (2 cups)
5 ounces spinach leaves, washed, dried,
    and sliced into strips

Cook the pasta 2 minutes less than the package directions indicate. (It will continue to soften as it marinates in the dressing.) Rinse with cold water, drain well, and set aside.

In a medium bowl, whisk together the mayonnaise, ¼ cup water, olive oil, rice vinegar, Parmesan, garlic, black pepper, salt, hot sauce, and cloves. Fold the pasta into the dressing and refrigerate for 1 hour.

Before serving, fold the bell pepper, mozzarella, and spinach leaves into the pasta. Serve chilled.

MAKE AHEAD This salad may be refrigerated for up to 2 days, but because the spinach tends to wilt, add it just before serving.

Marcella Rosene

Marcella Rosene was the cofounder, along with her husband, Harvey, of Pasta & Co, a small chain of neighborhood gourmet food and take-out shops in the Seattle area that we bought in 2000. Marcella set a new standard for gourmet food in Seattle when she opened her first store in Queen Anne neighborhood in 1980 and became the local tastemaker in introducing new foods to the local market. Marcella's dedication to wonderful food and her transformation from someone with a dream to the owner of a successful business is a true inspiration.

"We had no retail and no food experience, but I was an aspiring home cook," Marcella recalls. "We knew we would only open with the best location, which was University Avenue. We tried to get considered for a [space in a] mall, and they turned us down." Lucky for her they did, because Marcella and Harvey's first store was soon packed with customers, and they expanded to four more Seattle locations.

The concept for Pasta & Co was simple: Marcella and Harvey would make and sell fresh pasta and offer a full menu of upscale, high-quality take-out food, from appetizers to desserts. With inspiration from customers and employees, Pasta & Co was soon booming, and added a retail section of gourmet products. "I realized I could be a tastemaker, that we could spread a message," she says. Marcella remembers they were the first in Seattle to spur the sun-dried tomato craze— sun-dried tomato was *the* ingredient of the 1980s. Marcella will never forget meeting Giorgio DeLuca, partner of the famous Dean & DeLuca in New York City, when he visited Pasta & Co to view the store.

After twenty years in the business and three cookbooks to their name, Marcella and Harvey decided to sell the business. Choosing the right person to carry on the legacy was critical to Marcella. After talking to many potential owners, they sold Pasta & Co to us. "We sensed that Kurt was someone who, in his own way, is as enthused and consumed by the products and the business as we were," says Marcella. "When I sit across the table from him six years later, he is smitten. Kurt really evolved the business. I felt I infected him with our enthusiasm about the food," she adds.

POLKA DOT PASTA SALAD

SERVES 4 TO 6

THIS HEALTHY, LIGHT, AND COLORFUL PASTA SALAD, a longtime Pasta & Co favorite, makes a quick lunch and is a welcome addition to any picnic basket. The bright colors of the vegetables remind us of polka dots.

1^1/$_3$ cups orzo

6 tablespoons extra-virgin olive oil

1^1/$_2$ teaspoons grated lemon zest

^{1}/$_4$ cup freshly squeezed lemon juice (1 to 2 lemons)

2 garlic cloves, minced

1 teaspoon kosher salt, or more to taste

^{1}/$_4$ teaspoon freshly ground black pepper, or more to taste

Pinch of cayenne pepper

3 plum tomatoes, diced

1 small yellow squash, halved, seeded, and diced

^{1}/$_2$ cucumber, halved, seeded, and diced

2 green onions (white and green parts), thinly sliced

^{1}/$_4$ cup chopped fresh basil

2 tablespoons chopped fresh flat-leaf parsley

^{1}/$_2$ cup toasted slivered almonds (page 195)

Cook the orzo for 1 minute less than package instructions indicate. Rinse with cool water, drain well, and set aside.

In a large bowl, combine the olive oil, lemon zest, lemon juice, garlic, salt, black pepper, and cayenne. Add the cooked orzo and stir to coat.

Add the tomatoes, squash, cucumber, green onions, basil, and parsley to the orzo mixture and toss to combine. Taste for seasoning and add salt and freshly ground pepper as needed.

Top with the toasted almonds and serve chilled or at room temperature.

MAKE AHEAD To save time, the orzo mixture can be made 1 day in advance and combined with the vegetables just before serving.

PASTA
& GRAINS

PASTA AUBERGINE

VELVETY EGGPLANT, that beloved summer vegetable, comes to life in this easy pasta sauce. If you're short on time, you can make the sauce ahead; it tastes even better the next day. For a more substantial dish, serve it with your favorite Italian-style chicken sausage. A short, sturdy pasta like rigatoni, rotini, or penne is the best choice for this chunky sauce.

1 medium eggplant (approximately 1 pound), trimmed and cut into 3/4-inch cubes

1/4 cup extra-virgin olive oil

1/2 medium yellow onion, chopped

1 teaspoon packed light brown sugar

3 garlic cloves, minced

1/2 teaspoon House Herbs (page 233) or other Italian herb blend

1/2 teaspoon kosher salt

Pinch of red pepper flakes

2 bay leaves

1/2 cup white wine

1 28-ounce can diced tomatoes in juice

2 tablespoons capers, drained

10 ounces rigatoni (about 4 cups)

Preheat the oven to 400°F.

In a roasting pan, toss the eggplant with the olive oil. Scatter the onion over the eggplant and sprinkle the brown sugar on top. Bake for about 45 minutes, stirring twice to prevent the edges from browning.

While the eggplant is baking, combine the garlic, herbs, salt, red pepper flakes, bay leaves, white wine, and diced tomatoes in a medium bowl.

After 45 minutes, reduce the oven temperature to 350°F.

Remove the roasting pan from the oven and stir the tomato mixture into the roasted eggplant. Cover the pan tightly with foil and bake for an additional 1½ hours. The eggplant should be very tender. Remove the pan from the oven and stir in the capers. Let the eggplant cool, uncovered, for 5 minutes. Remove the bay leaves.

Cook the pasta according to package directions and toss with the sauce. Serve warm.

MAKE AHEAD The sauce can be refrigerated for up to 5 days. Once combined, the dish can be refrigerated for 1 day and then reheated in a 350°F. oven for 30 minutes.

LEMON RISOTTO

SERVES 4 AS A MAIN COURSE, 6 AS AN APPETIZER

RISOTTO IS A SIMPLE, ELEGANT DISH that acts as a vehicle for a variety of flavors. Adding lemon to risotto is common in Italy, where the subtly flavored dish is often served as an appetizer. I like it as a side to Butter-Rubbed Salmon (page 103) with Blueberry Sauce (page 104) or simply enjoy it as a vegetarian main course, perhaps accompanied by blanched asparagus.

5$\frac{1}{2}$ to 6 cups Chicken Stock (page 230) or store-bought low-sodium chicken or vegetable broth
2 tablespoons unsalted butter
1$\frac{1}{2}$ tablespoons extra-virgin olive oil
1 small yellow onion, minced
$\frac{1}{2}$ teaspoon kosher salt, or more to taste
2 cups Arborio rice
1 cup dry white wine

5 ounces Parmesan or other hard cheese (page 23), grated (1$\frac{1}{4}$ cups)
1 tablespoon chopped fresh flat-leaf parsley or 1 teaspoon dried
1 tablespoon grated lemon zest
2 tablespoons freshly squeezed lemon juice
Freshly ground white pepper, to taste

In a medium saucepan, bring the stock to a simmer over medium heat. Reduce the heat as low as possible to keep the stock warm until you are ready to use it.

In a large, heavy-bottomed, nonreactive skillet at least 10 inches wide, heat the butter and olive oil over medium heat. Add the onion and the salt. Sauté for 8 to 10 minutes, stirring frequently, until the onion has softened.

Add the rice to the skillet and cook for 3 minutes, stirring frequently to coat the rice with oil. Add the white wine and cook for 2 to 3 minutes, stirring frequently, until the wine is almost absorbed. Ladle 1$\frac{1}{2}$ to 2 cups of the hot stock over the rice. Stir frequently until all of the liquid is absorbed and your stirring spoon leaves a trail showing where it ran across the bottom of the pot. Ladle in another 1$\frac{1}{2}$ cups of liquid and stir until it is absorbed. Continue adding stock until the rice grains are al dente, about 30 minutes total. (You might not use all the stock.) If you prefer a softer risotto, add more stock until it has the desired consistency.

Stir in the Parmesan, parsley, lemon zest, and lemon juice. Taste for seasoning and add salt and pepper as needed. Serve immediately.

Cheese might just be the most versatile ingredient around. It can stand on its own or act as a garnish, a sauce, a textural element, a background flavor—cheese practically begs for creative cooks. Any kind of cheese can be tossed into a dish, whether it's leftover sliced cheese or chunks from a cheese plate. And incorporating different types of cheese in dishes can yield fabulous flavor combinations.

Here are a few tips before you start cooking.

- Melting cheese: Three factors affect how cheese melts: its fat content, its age, and how it is cut. Cheeses that are higher in fat, such as Brie, Cheddar, and Gouda, tend to melt more easily than lower-fat cheeses, such as low-fat mozzarella. Aged cheeses can withstand a higher temperature than younger cheeses, but the texture may be grainier when melted. Younger cheeses melt at low temperatures and become creamy and smooth. Finally, cut and prepare your cheese according to how you want it to melt. If you want a dense layer of melted cheese, as for the Toasted Tomato-Basil Sandwich (page 27), slice the cheese before melting. For quick, even melting, grate the cheese before adding it to a dish. A good rule of thumb: The harder the cheese, the smaller the grate. Similarly, chopped cheese melts more evenly than uneven chunks.

- Aged cheeses tend to be salty, so add salt to the recipe only at the end so you can more accurately gauge the salt level of the final dish.

- Cold cheese is easier to slice, grate, or crumble than room-temperature cheese. We stick fresh mozzarella and other gooey cheeses in the freezer for 20 minutes prior to slicing or grating.

- When cooking cheese on the stove for a cheese sauce, cook it over low to medium heat. Cooking cheese over high heat can cause it to separate. A béchamel or white sauce is a great way to incorporate cheese without having it break, because the flour in the béchamel holds the fat.

- Cooking with fresh cheeses can be tricky. While cream cheese is often added to baked goods and ricotta is the star of most lasagne dishes, fresh cheeses usually work best in cold dishes. If you do want to add a fresh cheese to a sauce, add it at the last minute to avoid breaking the sauce.

- A good rule of measurement for grated cheese: 8 ounces cheese makes about 2 cups grated.

THREE-GRAIN RISOTTO

SERVES 4 AS A MAIN COURSE, 6 AS A SIDE DISH

RISOTTO ISN'T LIMITED TO RICE. Here, toasted barley and orzo are included with the Arborio rice, adding great flavors and textures to the standard risotto. Toasting the barley is a key step to achieving its maximum flavor. This hearty dish is the perfect accompaniment to meat and poultry dishes, and it makes a satisfying vegetarian main course as well.

5 cups Chicken Stock (page 230) or
    store-bought low-sodium chicken or
    vegetable broth
1/2 cup pearl barley
2 tablespoons extra-virgin olive oil
1 small leek, chopped
2 garlic cloves, minced
1/2 cup Arborio rice

1 cup white wine
1/2 cup orzo
1 ounce Parmesan or other hard cheese
    (page 23), shredded (1/4 cup)
1/2 teaspoon kosher salt, or more to taste
1/2 teaspoon freshly ground pepper
2 ounces fresh goat's-milk cheese
    (1/4 cup)

In a medium saucepan, bring the stock to a simmer over medium heat. Reduce the heat as low as possible to keep the stock warm until you are ready to use it.

In a large, heavy-bottomed, nonreactive skillet at least 10 inches wide, toast the barley over medium-high heat, stirring frequently, until it smells nutty, about 5 minutes. Transfer the toasted barley to a small bowl and set aside.

In the same skillet, heat the olive oil over medium-high heat. Add the leek and garlic and sauté for 1 minute until the leek starts to soften.

Add the barley and Arborio rice and cook for 3 minutes, stirring frequently, to coat the rice. Add the white wine and cook for 2 to 3 minutes, stirring frequently, until the wine is almost absorbed. Ladle 1 1/2 to 2 cups of the hot stock over the rice. Stir frequently until all of the liquid is absorbed and a stirring spoon leaves a trail showing where it ran across the bottom of the pot. Ladle in an additional 1 1/2 cups of liquid and stir until the liquid is absorbed.

Add the orzo and continue adding stock until the grains are al dente, about 30 minutes total. If you prefer a softer risotto, add more stock until it has the desired consistency. (You might not use all the stock.)

Remove the pot from the heat and stir in the Parmesan until it is melted and completely incorporated. Taste for seasoning and add salt and pepper as needed. Serve immediately, topping each portion with a dollop of fresh goat cheese.

NOTE For tips on cleaning a leek, see page 24.

SCALLOP ORZO
with Wild Mushrooms and Sherry

SERVES 4

BRINY SCALLOPS AND WOODSY MUSHROOMS are tied together with the light, sweet note of sherry in this creamy fall pasta dish. We prefer hedgehog mushrooms because of their small size, but you could substitute other wild mushrooms if you prefer.

1½ cups orzo	⅔ cup pale dry sherry
4 tablespoons (½ stick) unsalted butter	1½ teaspoons whole-grain mustard
1 tablespoon extra-virgin olive oil	1 cup Chicken Stock (page 230) or store-bought low-sodium chicken broth
4 ounces hedgehog mushrooms or other wild mushrooms, roughly chopped	⅔ cup heavy cream
3 garlic cloves, minced	3 ounces hard cheese (page 23), shredded (¾ cup)
1 large shallot, chopped	12 sea scallops, side muscle removed, rinsed and patted dry
4 tablepoons fresh thyme	
Kosher salt	
Freshly ground black pepper	

Cook the orzo according to package instructions. Rinse with cool water, drain well, and set aside.

In a large skillet over medium-high heat, melt 2 tablespoons of the butter with the olive oil. Add the mushrooms, garlic, shallot, and 3 tablespoons of the fresh thyme. Season with ¼ teaspoon salt and ¼ teaspoon pepper. Sauté for 30 seconds.

Add the sherry and mustard. Cook for 20 seconds while stirring to deglaze the skillet. Add the chicken stock and heavy cream. Cook until the liquid is reduced by one-third, about 10 minutes. Reduce the heat to low and fold in the cheese. Cook until the cheese is completely melted, less than 1 minute. Remove the skillet from the heat, cover, and set aside.

In a separate medium skillet over medium-high heat, melt the remaining 2 tablespoons butter until it begins to brown, about 2 minutes. Sprinkle both sides of each scallop with salt and pepper. Lay the scallops in the pan. Cook the scallops for 2 minutes without moving them and then flip them. (The cooked side should be brown and crispy.) Cook the scallops for an additional 1 to 2 minutes. Be careful not to overcook them; the center of the scallop should remain translucent. Depending on the size of the pan, you may need to cook the scallops in batches. Remove the pan from the heat and set aside.

Add the orzo to the cream sauce in the skillet and return to medium heat. Remove from the heat when hot throughout.

To serve, divide the pasta evenly among 4 bowls. Place 3 scallops in each bowl and garnish with the remaining fresh thyme.

OLIVE OIL–POACHED PRAWNS
over Capellini

SERVES 4 TO 6

POACHING SEAFOOD IN OIL locks in its moisture and produces tender, juicy results. Here, adding fresh red snapper along with the prawns adds a textural contrast, but you could use either one, doubling the quantity. The oil from the poached seafood makes a flavorful sauce when studded with basil, tomatoes, and lemon zest. Delicate capellini, also known as angel hair pasta, rounds out an easy summer lunch or light supper.

1 cup extra-virgin olive oil

5 garlic cloves, smashed and roughly chopped

1 bunch fresh basil, roughly chopped, stems reserved

1/4 teaspoon red pepper flakes

3 tablespoons rice vinegar

1 pint cherry tomatoes, halved

Grated zest and juice of 2 lemons

1/4 red onion, roughly chopped (1/2 cup)

8 ounces skinless snapper fillet, cut into 1/2-inch pieces

1 pound 16–20-count prawns, peeled and deveined

2 1/4 teaspoons kosher salt, or more to taste

1/4 teaspoon freshly ground black pepper, or more to taste

12 ounces capellini (angel hair pasta)

1 cup roughly chopped fresh flat-leaf parsley

Bring a large pot of salted water to a boil.

In a large skillet over medium heat, heat the olive oil. Add the garlic cloves and half the basil, including the stems, and cook for 5 minutes. Using a slotted skimmer, remove the solids from the olive oil and discard.

Add the red pepper flakes, rice vinegar, about half of the cherry tomatoes, the lemon juice, and half of the onion to the skillet. Cook for 5 minutes. Add the snapper and prawns and season with the salt and pepper. Stir to coat the seafood with the oil. Arrange the seafood in a single layer in the olive oil, making sure it is completely submerged. Cook for 4 minutes; then, using tongs, flip the snapper and prawns and cook for 2 more minutes. The seafood is done when the snapper is opaque and the prawns are pink. Remove from the heat.

While the seafood is cooking, cook the pasta in the boiling water according to package directions. Transfer the pasta to a large bowl.

Add the parsley, the remaining fresh basil leaves, the lemon zest, and the remaining cherry tomatoes and red onions to the pasta. Pour the hot oil and seafood over the top and toss. (The fresh herbs should wilt from the heat of the pasta and oil.) Let sit for 1 minute and then toss again until all of the oil is absorbed by the pasta. Taste for seasoning and add more salt and pepper as needed.

Serve warm or at room temperature.

WINE AND FOOD PAIRING

Nothing completes a meal like a glass of wine, and while much has been written about wine and food pairing, I have a few suggestions of my own. I love wine and I believe it can enhance a dish, but wine and food pairing is a game of give and take. Ultimately there are no real rules, so be open to variation and experimentation.

Rules like "red wine with meat, white wine with fish" no longer apply when working with today's fusion of global flavors. A Pinot Noir can pair perfectly with grilled swordfish, while rich white varietals can be beautiful accompaniments to pork. (Frankly, with some more complicated dishes, the best pairing is a craft beer, but that's another story.)

Serve red wine at 65°F. and white wine at 50°F. (If wine is too warm, it will accentuate the alcohol in the wine, and if a wine is too cold, it can dull the flavors.) Use glasses with a wide bowl to allow plenty of room to swirl so you can enjoy the aromas of the wine. Avoid colored wineglasses; they prevent you from seeing the true color of the wine.

Ideally, wine should be stored at 55°F. If you achieve this optimal condition, pull both red and white wines half an hour before you want to drink them. Place the red wine on the countertop and the white wine in the refrigerator to bring them to the right serving temperature.

Here are some basic pairing principles to get you started:

- The wine should be equal to or higher in acid than the dish.

- The wine shouldn't overwhelm the food, and vice versa. The weight of the wine and the food is crucial. You wouldn't serve a big, oaky Chardonnay with a delicate pasta dish, just as a spicy tomato sauce would overwhelm a delicate Pinot Noir.

- Spicy foods need aromatic wines (or a craft beer). For Thai or Chinese food, look for slightly sweeter white varietals that have floral aromas such as Riesling, Viognier, or Gewürztraminer. Or try rosé; dry and fruity, it pairs with almost any dish.

- Sparkling wine is a great choice because it is versatile and pairs with many types of food. It's a great go-to choice when you're stumped; just make sure to buy dry sparkling instead of sweet. It's also the only type of wine that will pair with a dish that has a lot of vinegar or vinaigrette.

- Foods that have a salty, sour, or bitter taste will make wine seem sweeter and less tannic.

- Crisp white wines, such as Sauvignon Blanc, can cut through salty foods, such as olives and feta cheese.

- When pairing dessert wines with desserts, remember that sweet food makes sweet wine taste less sweet, so make sure the wine is sweeter than the food.

"WORLD'S BEST" MAC AND CHEESE

SERVES 4 AS A SIDE DISH

WE CAME UP WITH THIS RECIPE WHEN WE OPENED BEECHER'S. We wanted to show our customers that you can cook with and eat great cheese every day, and this killer mac and cheese uses two of our cheeses with a background hint of garlic powder and chipotle pepper. We've already won the vote for Seattle's best Mac and Cheese, but the 17,234 people a year from all over the world who eat it in our store tell us it's the world's best. This recipe serves about four people as a side dish. It doesn't look like a lot, but one bite of this creamy dish will show you why. If you double the recipe, bake it in a 9 x 13-inch pan for 30 minutes.

6 ounces penne

2 cups Beecher's Flagship Cheese Sauce (recipe follows)

1 ounce Cheddar, grated ($^1/_4$ cup)

1 ounce Gruyère cheese, grated ($^1/_4$ cup)

$^1/_4$ to $^1/_2$ teaspoon chipotle chili powder (see Note)

Preheat the oven to 350°F. Butter or oil an 8-inch baking dish.

Cook the penne 2 minutes less than package directions. (It will finish cooking in the oven.) Rinse the pasta in cold water and set aside.

Combine the cooked pasta and the sauce in a medium bowl and mix carefully but thoroughly. Scrape the pasta into the prepared baking dish. Sprinkle the top with the cheeses and then the chili powder.

Bake, uncovered, for 20 minutes. Let the mac and cheese sit for 5 minutes before serving.

NOTE One-half teaspoon of chipotle chili powder makes a spicy mac, so make sure your family and friends can handle it!

The proportion of pasta to cheese sauce is crucial to the success of the dish. It will look like a lot of sauce for the pasta, but some of the liquid will be absorbed.

MAKE AHEAD This recipe can be assembled before baking and frozen for up to 3 months—just be sure to use a freezer-to-oven pan and increase the baking time to 50 minutes.

Beecher's Flagship Cheese Sauce

MAKES ABOUT 4 CUPS

This was the first recipe we came up with for Beecher's. It was created specifically for the mac and cheese, but then we realized we could use the sauce in all sorts of dishes: Mix it with a little white wine for a rich fondue sauce, spoon it over poached eggs (see Poached Eggs with Cheese Sauce, page 214), or pour it over steamed broccoli for an easy veggie dish. You can experiment with other leftover cheeses to create new flavor combinations.

$1/4$ cup ($1/2$ stick) unsalted butter
$1/3$ cup all-purpose flour
3 cups milk
14 ounces semihard cheese (page 23), grated (about $3^1/2$ cups)

2 ounces semisoft cheese (page 23), grated ($1/2$ cup)
$1/2$ teaspoon kosher salt
$1/4$ to $1/2$ teaspoon chipotle chili powder
$1/8$ teaspoon garlic powder

Melt the butter in a heavy-bottomed saucepan over medium heat and whisk in the flour. Continue whisking and cooking for 2 minutes.

Slowly add the milk, whisking constantly. Cook until the sauce thickens, about 10 minutes, stirring frequently. Remove from the heat.

Add the cheeses, salt, chili powder, and garlic powder. Stir until the cheese is melted and all ingredients are incorporated, about 3 minutes. Use immediately, or refrigerate for up to 3 days.

This sauce reheats nicely on the stove in a saucepan over low heat. Stir frequently so the sauce doesn't scorch.

MARIACHI MAC AND CHEESE

SERVES 4 TO 6

THIS IS THE SAME GREAT BEECHER'S MAC AND CHEESE recipe taken to a new level, with the spice of chiles and the addition of vegetables. Feel free to experiment with left-over cheeses for new flavor combinations.

8 ounces penne

2 tablespoons ($^1/_4$ stick) unsalted butter

$2^1/_2$ tablespoons all-purpose flour

$1^1/_2$ cups milk

9 ounces sharp Cheddar, grated ($2^1/_4$ cups)

1 ounce Gruyère cheese, grated ($^1/_4$ cup)

$2^1/_2$ teaspoons finely minced chipotle peppers in adobo sauce (about 1 pepper; see Note)

1 4-ounce can diced green chiles, rinsed, or 3 roasted Anaheim chiles

$^3/_4$ teaspoon garlic powder

$1^1/_4$ teaspoons kosher salt

1 tablespoon extra-virgin olive oil

$^1/_2$ medium red onion, diced

1 cup cauliflower florets

$^1/_2$ medium red bell pepper, diced

$^1/_2$ cup fresh or frozen corn kernels

$^1/_4$ teaspoon paprika

Preheat the oven to 350°F. Butter or oil an 8-inch baking dish.

Cook the penne 2 minutes less than package directions. (It will finish cooking in the oven.) Rinse the pasta in cold water and set aside.

In a heavy-bottomed saucepan over medium heat, melt the butter and whisk in the flour. Continue whisking and cook for 2 minutes. Slowly add the milk, whisking constantly. Cook until the sauce thickens, about 8 minutes, stirring frequently. Remove from the heat. Add three-quarters of the Cheddar, the Gruyère, chipotle pepper, green chiles, garlic powder, and salt. Stir until the cheese is melted. Set aside.

In a medium skillet, heat the olive oil over medium-high heat. Add the onion, cauliflower, and bell pepper. Cook for 3 to 4 minutes, or until the onion is just beginning to brown. Remove from the heat and add the vegetables to the cheese sauce along with the corn. Fold the sauce into the cooked pasta. Pour the mixture into the prepared baking dish. Sprinkle with the remaining Cheddar cheese and the paprika.

Bake, uncovered, for 35 minutes, or until golden brown and bubbly. Let the mac and cheese rest for 5 minutes before serving.

NOTE Chipotle peppers in adobo sauce come in 7-ounce cans and can be found at most grocery stores. The peppers are very soft and become a pulp when finely minced. They are also spicy, so to reduce the spice of the mac and cheese, add less chipotle. Store leftover chipotle peppers in the refrigerator.

MAKE AHEAD This dish can be assembled before baking and then frozen up to 3 months ahead—just be sure to use a freezer-to-oven pan and increase the baking time to 50 minutes.

DUNGENESS CRAB MAC AND CHEESE

SERVES 4

THIS IS A TRULY DECADENT DISH, but you won't want to save it for special occasions. Adding another Pacific Northwest flavor to our classic mac and cheese was easy; the base is a cheese sauce made from flavorful crab stock, and cauliflower balances the sweet crab flavor.

6 ounces penne

$1/2$ pound cooked lump crabmeat, preferably Dungeness, rinsed and drained ($1^{1}/2$ cups)

5 tablespoons unsalted butter

1 cup roughly chopped cauliflower

1 ear fresh corn, kernels removed, or $2/3$ cup frozen corn kernels

3 tablespoons roughly chopped celery (about 1 rib)

$1/4$ teaspoon kosher salt

1 teaspoon capers, drained

Dash of cayenne pepper

$1/8$ teaspoon chili powder

Dash of turmeric

2 tablespoons all-purpose flour

$1^{1}/2$ cups Crab Stock (page 232)

1 tablespoon pale dry sherry

$1/2$ teaspoon chopped fresh tarragon

$1/2$ teaspoon freshly ground black pepper

6 ounces semihard cheese (page 23), shredded ($1^{1}/4$ cups)

1 ounce hard cheese (page 23), chopped (3 tablespoons)

3 tablespoons fresh bread crumbs

Heat oven to 375°F. Lightly oil an 8-inch baking dish.

Cook the penne 2 minutes less than package directions. (It will finish cooking in the oven.) Rinse the pasta in cold water and set aside.

Put the crabmeat in a large bowl and pick through it with your hands, removing any pieces of shell.

In a large skillet over medium-high heat, melt 1 tablespoon of the butter. Add the cauliflower and cook for 1 minute without stirring. The cauliflower will just begin to brown on the bottom. Flip the cauliflower, add the corn, celery, and salt, and sauté for another minute. Transfer the vegetables to a small bowl.

In the same pan over medium-high heat, melt 1 tablespoon of the butter. Add the capers and sauté until they are brown, about 1 minute. Remove the pan from the heat and add the cayenne, chili powder, and turmeric. Stir to combine. Gently fold in the crabmeat until it is fully coated. Transfer to a small bowl and set aside.

In the same skillet, melt the remaining 3 tablespoons butter over medium heat. Whisk in the flour to create a roux. Cook for 2 minutes, stirring constantly, and then slowly whisk in the stock. Continue whisking until fully combined, about 30 seconds. Add the sherry, tarragon, and pepper and stir. Remove from the heat and stir in the semihard cheese until it is completely melted, about 30 seconds. Mix in the pasta, vegetables, and the hard cheese.

Very gently fold in all but ⅓ cup of the crabmeat. Pour the pasta into the baking dish and spread the reserved crabmeat over the top, pressing it slightly down into the mac and cheese. (If the crabmeat is left on top, it will dry out while it cooks.) Sprinkle the bread crumbs over the top of the dish.

Bake for 50 minutes, or until the cheese is bubbling around the edges and the internal temperature of the dish is 160°F. Let the mac and cheese sit for 15 minutes before serving.

FISH & SHELLFISH

DUNGENESS CRAB CAKES WITH TANGY RÉMOULADE

CRAB ENCHILADA CASSEROLE

BUTTER-STEAMED CLAMS

SPICY SEARED SCALLOPS

NORTHWEST CIOPPINO

ITALIAN STEAMED MUSSELS

SEARED SWORDFISH WITH CAPER-ONION SAUCE

SALMON POKE

SURF AND SURF: CEDAR PLANK–GRILLED SALMON AND HALIBUT
WITH PARSLEY AND DILL PESTO

BUTTER-RUBBED SALMON WITH BLUEBERRY SAUCE

POACHED FISH IN A LIGHT VINAIGRETTE

BREADED HALIBUT CHEEKS

DUNGENESS CRAB CAKES
with Tangy Rémoulade

SERVES 8 AS AN APPETIZER, 4 AS A MAIN COURSE

DUNGENESS CRAB CAKES ARE THE QUINTESSENTIAL SEATTLE DISH, and there is much debate around town about which restaurant makes the best. Some local chefs like to add unusual ingredients to their crab cakes, but our only twist is a bit of cheese, which adds richness without overpowering the crab. We use Dungeness for its sweet crab flavor, but blue crabmeat can be substituted. To minimize last-minute preparation, you can refrigerate the crab cakes for several hours before cooking. Allow them to come to room temperature, uncovered, for at least 15 minutes before cooking, as slightly warmer cakes hold together better during cooking. Serving the crab cakes over fresh spinach with a light vinaigrette completes a lunch or dinner.

2 to 3 tablespoons unsalted butter

1 green onion (white and green parts), thinly sliced

1 stalk celery, diced

$1/4$ red bell pepper, diced

1 pound (3 cups) cooked lump crabmeat, preferably Dungeness, rinsed and drained

1 to 2 large eggs

2 small garlic cloves, minced

1 teaspoon Worcestershire sauce

2 teaspoons Old Bay Seasoning

$1/4$ cup Basic Mayonnaise (page 234) or any store-bought mayonnaise

1 ounce semihard cheese (page 23), grated ($1/4$ cup)

$2^{1}/2$ cups finely ground fresh bread crumbs

Tangy Rémoulade (recipe follows)

Heat a large skillet over medium heat. Melt 1 tablespoon of the butter and add the green onion, celery, and bell pepper. Cook for 2 to 3 minutes, stirring gently, until just softened. Remove the vegetables from the pan to a small plate or bowl and allow them to cool.

Place the crabmeat in a medium bowl and pick through it with your hands, removing any pieces of shell. In a small bowl, beat together 1 egg and the garlic, Worcestershire sauce, Old Bay, and mayonnaise. Add the egg mixture and cooled vegetables to the crabmeat and combine gently but thoroughly with a spatula or wooden spoon. Add the cheese and bread crumbs to the crabmeat and gently mix with your hands until evenly combined.

Divide the crabmeat mixture into 8 equal parts (about $3/4$ cup each) and form with your hands into patties approximately $3/4$ inch thick, pressing very firmly so the cakes stick together. (Moistening your hands with water will help keep the crab from sticking to them.) If the cakes do not hold together, dump them back in the bowl, beat the second egg in a small bowl, and add half the egg. Mix thoroughly to combine and form the crab cakes again. Place the crab cakes on a plate until ready to cook.

Reheat the skillet over medium-high heat and add 1 tablespoon of the butter. Carefully place 4 crab cakes in the hot pan. Do not crowd them. Cook for 3 to 4 minutes on one side without touching them. When the crab cakes are lightly browned on the bottom, carefully turn them over with a wide spatula and cook for an additional 3 to 4 minutes, until the second side is lightly browned. Transfer the crab cakes to a plate lined with a paper towel to drain. Cook the remaining 4 crab cakes in the skillet, adding 1 more tablespoon butter, if needed.

Serve hot, topped with a spoonful of rémoulade.

Tangy Rémoulade

A cold mayonnaise-based sauce that originated in France, rémoulade is a traditional condiment for crab cakes in New Orleans. You can assemble this version, a quick blend of pantry items, at the last minute or a few hours ahead. Its vivid color and zesty flavor make it the best choice for accompanying delicate chilled foods such as poached chicken, white fish, and, of course, crab cakes.

¹/₄ cup ketchup

3 tablespoons sour cream

2 tablespoons Basic Mayonnaise (page 234) or any all-natural mayonnaise

2 tablespoons whole-grain mustard

1¹/₂ tablespoons capers, drained

1 tablespoon peeled and grated fresh horseradish or creamy store-bought prepared horseradish

4 to 6 dashes Tabasco or other hot sauce

Kosher salt and freshly ground black pepper to taste

In a small bowl, briskly whisk together the ketchup, sour cream, mayonnaise, mustard, capers, horseradish, hot sauce, salt, and pepper with a fork to combine thoroughly. Cover and refrigerate until ready to use, up to 1 day ahead.

crab

While more than 4,400 types of crab exist, in the culinary world the selection is limited to just a handful of species. Here are the most common types of crab you'll see in the market:

BLUE CRAB: This olive-green crab is $3^1/_2$ to $5^1/_2$ inches in size and found in the waters of the Atlantic. Its meat has a delicate, nutty flavor. Blue crabs are also eaten as soft-shell crabs. Blue crab is sold whole (cooked or frozen) or as picked meat, graded by size.

DUNGENESS: This brownish gray crab from the Pacific turns bright red when cooked. It has a large yield of what some say is the sweetest meat. About $1^1/_2$ to 4 pounds in size, these crabs are most often found whole (live or cooked) or as cooked lump meat. You can sometimes find frozen whole Dungeness crab.

KING CRAB: The largest of the crabs, red king crabs can grow up to 8 feet long and weigh 20 pounds, although most average about 6 pounds. Caught in Alaska and Russia, only the legs and claws are edible; the sweet white meat has a reddish hue. King crab is usually sold frozen in leg or claw portions.

PEEKYTOE CRAB: Once considered a throwaway by lobster fishers, the sweet, flaky meat of the Maine peekytoe (meaning "picked toes") is rising in popularity. Also known as bay crabs, these small crabs cannot be shipped live and instead are available only as lump crabmeat, all of which is picked by hand.

SNOW CRAB: The snow crab, also known as the rock crab or spider crab because of its spindly legs, is harvested in Alaska, Canada, and in the Atlantic Ocean. It is sold in clusters, claws, "snap 'n' eat" legs, and as lump crabmeat.

STONE CRAB: These oval, brownish-yellowish crabs, also known as moro crabs, are harvested in Florida from October through May. Only the claw meat, which is sweet and flaky, is eaten.

Dungeness crab is a true Pacific Coast food: It's found only in the Pacific Ocean, and it gets its name from the town of Dungeness, Washington. The local crab season is summer, and that's when my boys and I go crabbing almost every day, filling the round metal crab pots with raw chicken and dropping them in the cold water, returning the next day to see what we've caught. We never know just how many crabs will take the bait, and it's a family tradition to guess how many will be in each pot. Bringing our catch back to the kitchen and preparing for our feast is the best part. Because we never

know how much crab we'll get, we plan the meal after the catch. You just have to go with what you have. If you wanted to make crab cakes but find that you don't have enough meat, make something else: crab cocktail, crab soup, or Dungeness crab mac and cheese. If you adapt your dishes to the ingredients, cooking becomes a lot more relaxing and a lot more fun.

Dungeness crabs have been part of the Northwest's seafood heritage for the millennium. The dark brown crabs that are brought to market usually weigh 1 to 2 pounds and up and measure at least

6¼ inches across. By law, only the male crabs can be caught, and thanks to careful fishery management and high reproductive rates, Dungeness are among the most sustainable shellfish in the world.

If you've ever cooked a live crab and tasted the sweet meat, you'll know that steaming crabs yourself makes a big difference in the flavor. I realize I am very lucky—not everyone has the Pacific Ocean as their backyard. If you don't have access to live crabs, look for high-quality cooked lump crabmeat from Dungeness, blue, peekytoe, or snow crabs. *Lump crabmeat* refers to whole pieces of white meat from the body of the crab, while *flake* refers to white and dark meat from the body and claws of the crab. The crab should be in large pieces, not shredded, and should be refrigerated. Most specialty markets and grocery stores sell untreated crab, which is what you want.

Much of the cooked crabmeat sold in stores is now treated with calcium disodium EDTA, a preservative that helps retard crystal formation. The Food and Drug Administration (FDA) has placed this preservative on its priority list of additives to study, and Australia has already outlawed it. Canned crab usually has added preservatives, so check the label carefully. When using precooked crabmeat, taste it first to make sure it is not excessively salty. If it is, rinse the meat to get rid of some of the salt.

If you're using live crab, don't be shy in asking the fishmonger for crabs with all the legs and claws intact; that's where the meat is. It's important to keep them cool and moist until cooking by keeping the wrapped crabs in the refrigerator or covering them with wet newspaper.

Live crabs are rambunctious, but preparing them isn't as hard as it seems. You have a couple of options. First, you can bring a large pot of water to a rolling boil, drop in the crab, cover the pot, and cook for 20 minutes. But just as chefs have found alternate ways of quickly killing and cooking

lobsters to get the sweetest-tasting meat, I prefer to deliver a quick, fatal blow with a rolling pin to the breastplate on the underside of the crab. Then I prepare, steam, and shell the crab as follows. I find that cleaning the crab before you cook it results in the sweetest meat.

Reach among the legs to place your hands on either side of the body with your thumbs on the breastplate. Holding onto the crab, push your thumbs forward and pull the legs of the crab together, bending the crab in half. Then grip the crab firmly and open your arms to pull the halves apart, leaving the main outer shell intact. Hold the broken edge of both halves under running water or salt water to rinse the guts and pith away. Reserve the crab shells for crab stock. The crab is now ready to cook. Because this is a messy process, it's best to prepare the crabs over the sink if you can't clean them right on the beach or off the side of a boat.

When you steam instead of boil the meat, the crab is white, tender, and succulent, without any fishy aroma or slimy texture. Cook the crab by heating about 1 cup water in a large pot with a vegetable or pasta steamer insert. Over high heat, bring the water to a boil. Add the crab halves and steam them for about 10 to 15 minutes, depending on how many you're cooking, until the meat is opaque and the shells turn dark orange. Remove the steamed crab from the pot and set them aside to cool.

Once the crab has cooled, pick out the meat from the body, legs, and claws. Place the crabmeat in a bowl and pick through it by hand to ensure no shell is left in the meat. Try to keep the pieces as intact as possible. The crabmeat will keep, covered, in the refrigerator, for up to 3 days after you cook it. Three whole Dungeness crabs yield about 1½ pounds crabmeat.

CRAB ENCHILADA CASSEROLE

SERVES 4 TO 6

ALL SUMMER LONG we find thousands of uses for crab. Crab soup, crab salad, crab sandwiches—there's no dish that doesn't taste better with crab. We created this recipe with left-over Easiest Crab Salad (page 46), but if you can't get Dungeness crab, substitute blue crab, chopped prawns or bay shrimp, or even lobster in this recipe.

10 6-inch corn tortillas
1 7-ounce jar salsa verde (medium to hot)
1 7½-ounce container crème fraîche
1 teaspoon extra-virgin olive oil
Easiest Crab Salad (page 46)

8 ounces semihard cheese (page 23), grated (2 cups)
Kosher salt and freshly ground black pepper to taste

Preheat the oven to 375°F.

Using either a gas stove or a broiler, toast the tortillas over or under the flame until they are partially crisp and the edges are just blackened, about 30 seconds per side. The tortillas will burn easily, so check them often while they are toasting.

In a small bowl, combine the salsa verde and crème fraîche to make a creamy sauce. Set aside.

Drizzle the olive oil in the bottom of an 8-inch baking dish. Trim 3 to 4 tortillas to fit the contours of the baking dish and make one complete layer of tortilla over the bottom of the dish. On top of the tortillas, layer one-third of the crab salad, one-third of the cheese, and one-third of the sauce. Top with another layer of tortillas, another third of the crab salad, another third of the cheese, and another third of the sauce. Make one final layer of the remaining tortillas and tortilla trimmings, crab salad, and cheese. (You will have formed three layers in the dish.) Pour the remaining sauce over the top, making sure to cover any exposed crab or tortilla pieces. Sprinkle the top with salt and pepper.

Bake for 30 minutes, or until the edges are brown and bubbly and the casserole is hot throughout. Let rest for 5 minutes before serving.

MAKE AHEAD Once baked, the enchiladas can be stored in the refrigerator, covered, for up to 2 days.

BUTTER-STEAMED CLAMS

SMALL, TENDER, AND SWEET, MANILA CLAMS are the most tender of the Pacific Northwest clams, which also include Pacific littlenecks, geoducks, butter clams, and jackknife clams. Manila clams are available at most fish markets. Parsley and cilantro brighten the flavor of this dish, but any other fresh herb can be used, such as thyme, basil, or oregano.

1 cup Chicken Stock (page 230) or store-bought low-sodium chicken broth

1 cup white wine

2 garlic cloves, chopped

1/4 yellow onion, thinly sliced

1/4 cup roughly chopped fresh flat-leaf parsley

2 tablespoons roughly chopped fresh cilantro

1/2 teaspoon red pepper flakes

2 tablespoons freshly squeezed lemon juice

4 pounds Manila clams, scrubbed

4 tablespoons (1/2 stick) unsalted butter

1/2 teaspoon freshly ground black pepper

Pour the chicken stock and wine into a stockpot or a large pot and bring to a boil over high heat. Cook for 10 minutes or until the liquid is reduced to 1/4 cup. The last 2 minutes of the reduction goes quickly, so check often. The liquid will resemble a brown glaze. Remove the pan from the heat.

Add the garlic, onion, parsley, cilantro, red pepper flakes, and lemon juice to the pan and stir. Add the clams, cover the pan, and cook on high for 5 to 10 minutes, or until the clams open.

Remove the pan from the heat and discard any unopened clams. Add the butter and pepper, cover, and let sit until the butter melts, about 2 minutes. Toss gently.

Spoon the clams into bowls, spooning any liquid remaining in the pan over the top. Serve hot.

pacific northwest shellfish

Whether it's the Pacific Ocean or Puget Sound, a river or a stream, water is the lifeblood of the Pacific Northwest. While salmon and Dungeness crab get all the glory, fresh shellfish, such as clams, mussels, and Pacific oysters, are pulled right from the ocean and are celebrated in dishes throughout the region for their robust flavors and their short cooking times.

Puget Sound is a unique aquaculture, one of just two areas in the United States that provide the perfect climate for shellfish: a protected body of water. Because of this, and because the region is a gateway to the seafood bounty of Alaska, which includes shrimp and sea scallops, local markets offer dozens of types of shellfish.

OYSTERS: Washington State is a big producer of Pacific oysters, so you'll see them on restaurant menus and in home kitchens raw, fried, or barbecued. The mild-flavored Pacific oyster, the crisp Olympic, and the tiny Kumamoto are the most common of the fifteen-plus varieties of oyster harvested in the region. They are primarily farm-raised. Oysters are good in any season except summer, when they are spawning and have a less desirable, slightly gooey texture.

CLAMS: Pacific littlenecks, Manila clams, geoducks (pronounced gooey-ducks), butter clams, and jackknife clams provide plenty of inspiration for the Pacific Northwest cook. Clamming is a popular pastime on the Washington coast, with locals finding razor clams for their fifteen-clam limit.

MUSSELS: Seven species of freshwater mussel are native to the Pacific Northwest, including the popular Penn Cove mussel, considered the sweetest. Mediterranean mussels are a close second; both are available year-round. Steamed with garlic and white wine or added to soups and pastas, mussels provide a sweet, meaty element to any dish.

SHRIMP: Local shrimp season runs from December through April and yields small, red shrimp. Sweet Oregon Bay shrimp, also called pink shrimp, are another regional favorite, as are Alaskan shrimp. From the large Spot variety to the tiny Humpy, five varieties of shrimp thrive in Alaska's waters.

Storing live shellfish properly is crucial. Buy shellfish the day you plan to cook it, and place live oysters, clams, and mussels in a bowl and cover them with a damp towel and refrigerate until you cook them (don't cover them with ice). Shellfish needs to breathe, so don't keep it in plastic bags.

When buying frozen shellfish, look for the IQF (individual quick frozen) indicator. This process retains the integrity of the shellfish.

SPICY SEARED SCALLOPS

SERVES 4

THE MILD-FLAVORED PICKAPEPPA is my favorite brand of steak sauce. Made from a centuries-old recipe in Jamaica, Pickapeppa is completely natural and has just the right balance of smoky, sweet, and spicy flavors. It is particularly delicious when served with meaty scallops. Serve the scallops hot as a passed hors d'oeuvre or chilled as a light summer appetizer.

4 teaspoons extra-virgin olive oil

4 teaspoons Pickapeppa brand steak sauce

$1/2$ teaspoon freshly ground black pepper

$1/4$ teaspoon red pepper flakes

$1/4$ teaspoon cayenne pepper

$1/2$ teaspoon sea salt

16 sea scallops (about $1^1/2$ ounces each), side muscle removed, rinsed and patted dry

4 tablespoons ($1/2$ stick) unsalted butter

In a large bowl, combine the olive oil, steak sauce, black pepper, red pepper flakes, cayenne, and salt. Add the scallops to the bowl and gently toss. Set the bowl aside and let the scallops marinate for 10 minutes.

Melt the butter in a large skillet over medium-high heat until it begins to brown. Lay the seasoned scallops in the pan and cook without moving for $3^1/2$ minutes, or until the scallops are browned but not burned. Depending on the size of the pan, you may need to cook the scallops in batches. Using tongs or a spatula, turn the scallops over and cook for 1 more minute. Be careful not to overcook; the center of the scallop should remain translucent. Transfer the scallops to a plate and serve hot.

scallops

Two types of scallops are available in most markets: bay (1/2 to 1 inch in size) and sea scallops (1 1/2 to 2 inches in size). Day-boat scallops, which can be either type, have been caught on a boat that returns to shore within 24 hours and are not treated with any additives or preservatives. Fresh scallops are available October through March, and frozen scallops are available year-round. Diver scallops are yet another type of scallop; these are harvested in the ocean by hand and are more expensive than other types. The season for diver scallops in the Atlantic Ocean runs from November to April.

Because scallops are so perishable, they are often treated with additives to extend their shelf life. The scallops are caught and soaked in preservatives so they absorb water and last longer, and whiteners are used to achieve the bright white color. These scallops are labeled "treated," and if the amount of moisture exceeds 80 percent of the weight of the scallops, they fall into a separate product category that must be labeled "scallop product, water added." Because of their high water content, treated scallops may not brown or caramelize as well as untreated scallops during cooking, and the flavor is completely different. The result for the consumer, besides consuming a chemical, is paying for water that cooks off. Scallops labeled "dry," "dry-pack," "untreated," or "chemical-free" are fresh scallops that do not contain preservatives.

Regardless of whether they're day-boat, frozen, or fresh, *untreated* is the most important term to look for. When buying fresh scallops, look for an ivory or pinkish color, which indicates that a bleach or whitener has not been used. They should be odorless or have a slightly sweet scent. If you aren't sure about the quality of the fresh shellfish in your local fish market, buy frozen scallops instead. Scallops are also sold IQF in the frozen foods section. IQF scallops are often of higher quality than the fresh scallops sold in most grocery stores.

In the United States, scallops are almost always sold shucked. Sea scallops often have a large muscle on the side that should be removed before cooking. To prevent them from drying out and getting tough, cook scallops on high heat for short periods. Sautéing them in butter is another way to enjoy their sweet flavor.

NORTHWEST CIOPPINO

SERVES 6 TO 8

CIOPPINO, THE CLASSIC ITALIAN-AMERICAN FISH STEW for which San Francisco is famous, takes on a new life in the Northwest, with fennel and a hint of anchovy to boost the flavor. The mashed avocado is used as a thickener and adds a richness to the dish, but it's optional. We use a variety of seafood, but feel free to use whatever is fresh in your fish market. We like to use true cod, also known as Pacific cod, because of its flaky texture and mild flavor. (Pacific cod is preferable to Atlantic cod, an overfished species.) True cod is often available frozen. If you find it fresh ask your fishmonger to bone it for you.

1 tablespoon extra-virgin olive oil

6 garlic cloves, chopped

1 medium yellow onion, chopped

1/2 green bell pepper, chopped

2 8-ounce bottles clam juice

2 tablespoons freshly squeezed lemon juice

4 cups Marinara Sauce with Fresh Herbs (page 241) or store-bought marinara sauce

1/2 teaspoon kosher salt

1 teaspoon red pepper flakes (see Note)

1/4 teaspoon freshly ground black pepper, or more to taste

1/2 avocado, mashed

1 teaspoon anchovy paste

1/2 fennel bulb, cored and roughly chopped

8 ounces skinless cod or other meaty white fish fillet, cut into 1-inch cubes

5 ounces bay scallops

8 ounces large prawns, peeled and deveined

1 pound Manila clams, scrubbed

1 pound mussels, scrubbed and debearded

Heat the olive oil in a large pot over medium heat. Add the garlic, onion, and bell pepper and cook until the onion is just translucent, about 3 minutes. Add the clam juice and lemon juice and stir to combine. Add the marinara sauce, salt, red pepper flakes, black pepper, avocado, anchovy paste, and fennel and stir. Simmer the mixture for 5 minutes, stirring occasionally.

Carefully place the cod, scallops, prawns, clams, and mussels in the pot. Cover and cook over medium heat for about 5 minutes, or until the prawns turn pink and the clams and mussels open. Remove the pan from the heat, discarding any unopened clams and mussels.

Ladle the cioppino into large bowls, garnishing each with black pepper, if desired. Serve hot.

NOTE A full teaspoon of red pepper flakes makes the cioppino hot and spicy; if your guests are sensitive to spice, tone it down by adding just 1/2 teaspoon or less.

ITALIAN STEAMED MUSSELS

SERVES 4 AS AN APPETIZER, 2 AS A MAIN COURSE

A BEAUTIFUL BOWL OF FRESHLY STEAMED MUSSELS is even better with marinara sauce, with the tomato playing off the tender, salty shellfish. Serve this dish as a starter, or ladle the mussels over spaghetti for a hearty pasta dish. Be sure to serve a loaf of warm, crusty bread alongside to soak up the juices.

2 tablespoons extra-virgin olive oil

$1\frac{1}{2}$ ounces (2 to 3 slices) thinly sliced prosciutto, chopped

4 garlic cloves, minced

3 tablespoons thinly sliced sun-dried tomatoes in oil, drained

2 cups Marinara Sauce with Fresh Herbs (page 241) or store-bought marinara sauce

4 fresh sage leaves, thinly sliced (optional)

1 pound mussels, scrubbed and debearded

$\frac{1}{4}$ cup roughly chopped fresh flat-leaf parsley

Heat the olive oil in a stockpot or a large pot on medium-high heat. Add the prosciutto and sauté for 3 to 4 minutes, or until brown. Add the garlic and sun-dried tomatoes and sauté for 30 seconds.

Stir in the marinara sauce and sage and bring to a boil. Add the mussels, cover the pan, and cook on high heat for 3 to 5 minutes, or until the mussels open.

Remove the pan from the heat and discard any unopened mussels. Spoon the mussels and the sauce into 4 bowls, sprinkle with the parsley, and serve hot.

SEARED SWORDFISH
with Caper-Onion Sauce

SERVES 4

WITH A MEATY TEXTURE AND MILD FLAVOR, swordfish pairs flawlessly with bold ingredients. The caper-onion sauce, with bracing white wine and lemon, brings big flavor to the fish. If you can't find swordfish, substitute another meaty fish, such as mahi-mahi.

1/4 cup extra-virgin olive oil

1/4 medium yellow onion, thickly sliced lengthwise

2 tablespoons capers, drained

4 8-ounce swordfish steaks

Kosher salt and freshly ground black pepper to taste

1 garlic clove, minced

2 teaspoons freshly squeezed lemon juice

1 1/2 cups white wine

1 1/2 teaspoons sugar

2 tablespoons roughly chopped fresh basil

1 tablespoon cold unsalted butter, cut into pieces

Heat the oil in a large skillet over medium-high heat. Add the onion and sauté for 1 minute. Add the capers and sauté until the onions are just barely translucent, about 2 minutes. (Be careful when you add the capers; they may spit in the hot oil.) Push the vegetables to the side of the pan with a spatula.

Sprinkle both sides of each swordfish steak with a pinch each of salt and pepper. Lay the swordfish in the middle of the frying pan, leaving the onions pushed to the side. Cook the swordfish for 2 minutes. While the swordfish cooks, stir the vegetable mixture to prevent it from burning. Reduce the temperature to medium and flip the swordfish. Spoon the vegetable mixture on top of the swordfish. Cook the swordfish for 1 1/2 more minutes, or to desired level of doneness. For medium rare, a meat thermometer inserted in the thickest part of the swordfish will read 145°F. For medium to well done, cook the fish to 155°F. or higher. Remove the pan from the heat and transfer the swordfish to a serving platter, leaving the onion mixture in the pan.

Add the garlic, lemon juice, white wine, sugar, and a pinch each of salt and pepper to the onion mixture and stir. Bring to a boil over high heat and reduce the liquid to 1/4 cup, about 5 minutes. Remove from the heat, add the basil, and whisk in the butter until it melts.

Spoon the sauce over the swordfish and serve.

salmon

With so many types of salmon in the fish store, it can be a challenge to decide just which kind to buy. There are two types, or genus, of salmon: Atlantic salmon, which is usually farmed, and Pacific salmon, which is most often wild but is also found farmed. (For more information on wild and farmed fish, see "The Fish Debate: Farmed or Wild?," page 107.)

There are five species of Pacific salmon. Within these categories, some salmon are also labeled according to where they were caught, such as Copper River Salmon from the Copper River in Alaska.

CHINOOK, or king salmon, the largest and fattiest fish, has firm, red flesh.

CHUM, also called keta or dog salmon, is a lower-fat fish with firm, pale flesh and a very mild flavor. Chum is sold fresh, and the chum salmon fish eggs, or roe, are highly regarded.

COHO, or silver salmon, is a small fish with medium-red, less fatty flesh.

PINK, or humpback, is the leanest salmon. It has soft, pink flesh.

SOCKEYE, also called red or blueback, has deep red meat, a firm texture, and the second highest fat content. It has been found to have the highest levels of omega-3s of all the types of salmon.

All varieties except coho are usually available canned, commercially smoked, frozen, and fresh.

When purchasing salmon, look for firm flesh, clear eyes, and flat, shiny scales. According to one fishmonger we buy from, fresh fish should smell like high tide, not low tide. There is really little difference in flavor among the types of salmon; personal taste and cost are the two considerations.

Bruce Gore

There would be no Pacific Northwest cuisine without salmon, and one person is responsible for transforming the quality of salmon in the region. Bruce Gore, owner of Triad Fisheries, pioneered the idea of a humane, quality-driven process of flash-freezing fish as soon as it is caught, eliminating the need for preservatives or additives and delivering the highest-quality fish possible to the dinner table.

Starting the moment he landed a 44-pound king salmon with his dad on the Columbia River when he was eight years old, Bruce knew his future was in fish. He grew up in Longview, Washington, and spent his summers crewing on purseiners (a type of fishing boat) in Alaska. After college, Bruce bought his own boat and started his own fishing business. From the beginning, he made a commitment to a different kind of commercial fishing. "The salmon are the physical embodiment of the spirit and the essence of the Pacific Northwest people, and they need to be treated with reverence," says Bruce. "I felt I had a moral responsibility to generate the maximum value with the least amount of carnage. I always thought, 'These fish deserve better.'"

What sets Bruce apart from other fishermen is that his salmon are caught individually by hook and line (known as trolling) in southeast Alaska, and as soon as they are caught they are instantly killed with a blow to the head, eliminating any stress or struggle, which results in a higher-quality fish. The salmon are then processed and frozen within 15 to 90 minutes of capture. This is called Frozen-at-Sea (FAS), and Bruce began this revolutionary process thirty years ago. The key is immediate, rapid freezing at very low temperature (–40°F.), known as cryogenic freezing. This process produces fish with extremely low bacteria count, a long shelf life, and clarity of flavor. In addition, each fish from Bruce's fishery is 100 percent traceable to its source, a first for the seafood industry.

Bruce's first sale was to Ray's Boathouse in Seattle in 1978. The local support was crucial to his new venture. "'Frozen' and 'quality' were thought to be mutually exclusive, so it was necessary to find someone in the food business who was enlightened about what was being accomplished. We found that in Ray's Boathouse," says Bruce. Ray's Boathouse enjoyed instant success with their fish. The idea of "Fisherman Treats Fish Like Food" made the news, and culinary luminaries such as Julia Child featured Bruce's fish on television.

Bruce points out that sustainable fishery practices are crucial to maintaining the fish supply. "I started fishing in Alaska forty years ago, and the harvest for the whole state was 20 million salmon annually," he says. "Today the harvest is between 160 and 220 million annually. That is on a sustained basis, and that is totally due to good habitat and good sustainable management. Alaska is a huge success story, and that's why we fish there."

Today, Bruce's business includes a fleet of more than thirty boats, the fishery in Alaska, and an office in Bainbridge Island, Washington. His reputation for quality has led to an international enterprise: Bruce sells his products on three continents, and in Japan his salmon is considered the highest-grade sashimi in the world. He is also one of the few fishermen to sell salmon to Scotland, which is very selective and sets extremely high standards for their smoked salmon. Bruce also catches halibut, black cod, ling cod, albacore tuna, and spot prawns; these are available in top-notch restaurants and upscale grocery stores around the country.

SALMON POKE

WHILE THE NAME MAY SOUND FANCY, this is really a very simple dish, a sashimi salad brightened with freshly squeezed lime juice. Inspired by the Hawaiian fish dish, the addition of avocado acts as a color and texture counterpoint. The salmon should be frozen for at least 24 hours to kill any parasites that might be in the fish; it's also much easier to cut the fish while it's still partially frozen.

1 pound skinless sashimi-grade king salmon fillet, pin bones removed, cut into 1/4-inch cubes

7 tablespoons extra-virgin olive oil

2 tablespoons unpacked light brown sugar

1/2 to 3/4 teaspoon Tabasco or other hot sauce

Kosher salt and freshly ground black pepper to taste

2 ripe avocados, peeled and pitted

1 small shallot, minced

2 tablespoons freshly squeezed lime juice (1 lime)

3 tablespoons freshly squeezed lemon juice (1 to 2 lemons)

1 tablespoon champagne vinegar

1/4 cup sour cream

2 teaspoons chopped fresh dill

In a medium bowl, combine the salmon, 1 tablespoon of the olive oil, the brown sugar, and the hot sauce, salt, and pepper. Mix gently and then set aside for 5 minutes.

In a separate bowl, roughly chop—even lightly mash—the avocados. Mix in the shallot and lime juice. Set aside.

To make the dressing, whisk together the remaining 6 tablespoons olive oil, the lemon juice, and vinegar. Add salt and pepper to taste.

To serve, divide the avocado mix among 4 small plates. Pat the avocado down into a 3-inch circle in the center of the plates. Top with the salmon, a small dollop of sour cream, and some dill. Drizzle the dressing over the top and serve immediately.

SURF AND SURF:
CEDAR PLANK–GRILLED SALMON AND HALIBUT
with Parsley and Dill Pesto

SERVES 6

THIS IS A NORTHWEST TAKE ON THE CLASSIC SURF AND TURF, but instead of steak I like to include another fish. Halibut and salmon make a great combination because they have complementary flavors, cooking times, and thickness. (If you can get Alaskan halibut, even better.) Grilled on a cedar plank and served with fresh pesto, the fish have flavors that really pop. You can use any untreated cedar board to cook the fish. Cookware stores sell rather thick planks, but some big box hardware stores and large grocery stores sell thinner untreated cedar planks in the barbecue department.

1¼ pounds skin-on salmon fillets

1¼ pounds skin-on halibut fillets

1 tablespoon extra-virgin olive oil

Kosher salt and freshly ground black pepper to taste

Parsley and Dill Pesto (recipe follows)

Soak untreated cedar plank in water for at least 1 hour. Prepare your grill by scraping it, oiling it, and heating it to medium.

Carefully rinse and dry each fillet. If you feel any bones when you run your fingers along the fillet, you may wish to remove them. Using needlenose pliers or strong tweezers, gently pull out the bones in the same direction they grew to avoid damaging the fish.

Place the fish on the plank, brush them with olive oil, and season with salt and pepper. Place the plank over the flame or hot coals. It will burn, but this is normal and a part of the recipe. If you see open flames, turn the heat to low and spray the plank with a little bit of water from a spray bottle. You can also move it to a cooler part of the grill.

Cook until the juices turn opaque and solid on the top of the fish, approximately 10 minutes for each inch of thickness. Do not overcook. The meat thermometer should read 145°F. when inserted into the thickest part of the fish.

At this point, most of the plank will be charred around the fish. Remove the fish to a platter, leaving the skin on the plank, and discard the plank. Spoon the pesto over the fish before serving.

Parsley and Dill Pesto

MAKES 1 CUP

A great topping on fish, this fresh pesto also makes a wonderful pasta sauce or dipping sauce for bread. This recipe is a good excuse to experiment with different cheeses.

1 or 2 small garlic cloves, peeled
1 cup packed fresh flat-leaf parsley
½ cup packed fresh dill
2 tablespoons chopped preserved lemon
　　(see page 165) or 1 tablespoon grated
　　lemon zest

2 ounces semihard cheese (page 23),
　　grated (½ cup)
½ cup plus 2 tablespoons extra-virgin
　　olive oil
1 teaspoon kosher salt
½ teaspoon freshly ground black pepper

In a food processor or blender, blend the garlic. Add the parsley, dill, preserved lemon, cheese, olive oil, salt, and pepper and pulse until well combined. Scrape down the sides of the bowl and pulse until the mixture forms a smooth paste.

MAKE AHEAD The pesto will keep, covered, in the refrigerator for up to 5 days.

Tom Douglas

Ask anyone in Seattle who put Seattle on the culinary map, and undoubtedly the answer will be Tom Douglas. Besides being a great guy, restaurateur Tom Douglas makes great food that isn't fussy, which is typical of the Pacific Northwest. Between his obsession with local ingredients and the accessibility of his food, Tom is unquestionably a culinary icon.

Tom moved to Seattle in 1976 when he was nineteen. He became the chef at Café Sport in 1982, and it was there he discovered what it meant to cook locally. "To me, it was about recognizing the idea of cooking with local food," says Tom. "Café Sport focused on global food and regional ingredients, and that is when it occurred to me that using local ingredients would make a difference. Of course there were people around the country who championed the idea, like Julia Child and Alice Waters, and you started to recognize there was a reason people wanted to eat salmon when they came to the Pacific Northwest. Fishermen were learning how to catch salmon better, thanks to John Rawley, and learning how to process salmon better, thanks to Bruce Gore," notes Tom.

In 1989, Tom and his wife, Jackie Cross, opened their own restaurant, Dahlia Lounge. "When I opened Dahlia, I was given respect in the community because they saw me as a local. They gave me a shot," says Tom. From the beginning, he carried the notion of using ingredients grown close to home in his own restaurant. "Local is the number-one thing for me," he says. "We did that very early on, and local is more important than organic because it takes seven years for a farm to turn organic and you have to support the farmers while they're in the process. There's nothing like a farmer walking up to your back door." Tom recalls that this support had an unexpected twist. "It got so successful we ended up losing up our best farmers because grocery stores like PCC [Puget Consumers Co-op] were swooping in and telling the farmers, 'We will take everything you grow,'" he says. His philosophy was slowly spreading to restaurants throughout Seattle. "It's about making the change to when you don't have a good product not to serve it at all," notes Tom. "It's nice to see restaurants willing to make a decision not solely based on price. That's a big step. It's only worth it to me if the customers go along for the ride. If I'm interested, I can assume the customers are coming along with me."

Tom's cooking style has won him more than local acclaim. In 1994, he won the James Beard Association Award for Best Chef Northwest. In 1995, Tom and Jackie opened their second restaurant, Etta's Seafood, in Pike Place Market in the old Café Sport space. Palace Kitchen followed in 1996, and a fourth restaurant, Lola, opened in 2004.

It's been thirty years since Tom made his way to the Pacific Northwest, and with 450 employees, four hugely successful restaurants, and a bakery as well as a catering business, a line of spice rubs and marinades, three cookbooks, and a radio show, he's clearly the leader of the Seattle culinary pack—and customers are just as clearly going along for the ride.

BUTTER-RUBBED SALMON
with Blueberry Sauce

SERVES 6

SMOKED, POACHED, GRILLED, OR SAUTÉED, salmon is what's for dinner in the Northwest. Its rich flavor is even better when paired with a butter rub. If you prepare this dish in advance, bring the salmon to nearly room temperature before you cook it. Using a thicker piece of salmon will give you better cuts. Otherwise, if the butter rub is too cold, it will flake off the salmon. The sweet blueberry sauce provides an unexpected color and flavor contrast to the rub.

1 2-pound salmon fillet, skinned
Lemon-Caper Butter Rub (recipe follows)

Blueberry Sauce (recipe follows)

Remove the bones and cut the salmon fillet into 6 pieces at a 45-degree angle along the bias. Try to maintain uniform thickness in the slices, cutting wider pieces toward the narrower ends of the salmon and thinner pieces toward the thick center of the salmon.

Using a basting brush and about half of the butter rub, coat one side of the salmon pieces with the rub. Refrigerate the salmon for 5 minutes, or until the butter just hardens into a glaze.

Heat a large skillet or griddle over medium-high heat.

Lay the salmon pieces, butter-rub side down, in the pan and cook until the bottom half of the salmon flesh is opaque, about 3 minutes. Brush the remaining butter rub over the salmon and flip the pieces. Cook for 1 more minute. The salmon will be nearly opaque throughout but still very moist.

Serve hot, topped with blueberry sauce.

Lemon-Caper Butter Rub

MAKES ¹/₃ CUP

4 tablespoons (¹/₂ stick) unsalted butter, melted
1 teaspoon capers, drained and mashed
1 teaspoon packed grated lemon zest
¹/₂ teaspoon garlic powder

¹/₂ teaspoon House Herbs (page 233) or other Italian herb blend
1 tablespoon diced yellow onion
¹/₂ teaspoon kosher salt
¹/₄ teaspoon freshly ground black pepper

Whisk together the butter, capers, lemon zest, garlic powder, herbs, onion, salt, and pepper.

MAKE AHEAD Prepare the butter rub up to 1 week in advance.

Blueberry Sauce

MAKES 1¹/₂ CUPS

Pacific Northwesterners love their blueberries. From July to September, cartons of fresh blue-berries fill the grocery stores and farmer's markets. The most prized is the wild Mt. Rainier blueberry, which grows in the foothills of the Cascade Mountains in Washington State, but farms all over Oregon and Washington grow the bright blue fruit. Use fresh blueberries to make the sauce only if they're in season; otherwise, use frozen wild blueberries. The sweetness of the blueberries is a stark contrast to savory flavors, and when drizzled over meat or fish, the sauce takes on another level of richness.

2 cups Chicken Stock (page 230) or store-bought low-sodium chicken broth
¹/₄ medium yellow onion
¹/₄ sweet apple, such as Fuji
3 to 4 sprigs fresh thyme
2 cups fresh or frozen blueberries

1¹/₂ teaspoons freshly squeezed lemon juice
¹/₄ teaspoon kosher salt
¹/₄ teaspoon freshly ground black pepper
3 tablespoons unsalted butter, cut into ¹/₂-inch pieces

In a small saucepan, bring the chicken stock to a boil. Reduce the heat to medium and add the onion, apple, and thyme. Simmer for 30 minutes, stirring occasionally, turning over the onion and the apple, until the stock is reduced by half.

With a slotted spoon, remove the onion, apple, and thyme from the stock and discard. Add the blueberries and bring to a boil. Reduce the heat to medium-low and simmer for 20 minutes, or until the liquid is reduced to ³/₄ cup.

Remove the pan from the heat. Add the lemon juice, salt, and pepper and stir. Add the butter and whisk the sauce until the butter is completely melted, about 1 minute. Serve hot.

MAKE AHEAD The sauce will keep for 7 days in the refrigerator and can be gently reheated over low heat before serving.

POACHED FISH
in a Light Vinaigrette

SERVES 4 TO 6

THE DELICATE FLAVORS OF COD shine when the fish is cooked in a light and flavorful broth. Served chilled, it is perfect for a warm summer evening. When the cod is served with a grain or plain steamed rice, the vinaigrette becomes the sauce.

2 pounds firm, white fish fillet, such as true cod (also known as Pacific cod), ling cod, halibut, or snapper, skinned and bones removed
Light Vinaigrette (recipe follows)

1 small fennel bulb, halved, cored, and thinly sliced
1 large beefsteak tomato, diced
2 tablespoons thinly sliced fresh basil

Carefully rinse and dry the fish. If you feel any bones when you run your fingers along the fillet, you may wish to remove them. Using needlenose pliers or strong tweezers, gently pull out the bones in the same direction they grew so as not to damage the fish.

Fill a large, shallow straight-sided pan or a roasting pan with 2½ inches water. Bring the water to a simmer on high heat and then reduce the heat to medium. Add the fish and simmer gently until it just begins to flake when prodded with a knife, about 7 to 8 minutes for a 1-inch-thick fillet. (Remember: The fish will continue to cook after you remove it from the pan.) Transfer the fish carefully with a spatula to a large, shallow, nonreactive serving dish.

Pour the dressing over the poached fish and refrigerate for at least 2 hours or up to 2 days.

To serve, arrange the fennel, tomato, and basil on top of the fish. Serve chilled or at room temperature.

Light Vinaigrette

MAKES ABOUT 1 CUP

¼ cup rice vinegar
2 tablespoons freshly squeezed lemon juice
1 teaspoon kosher salt
1 teaspoon freshly ground black pepper

¾ teaspoon dried basil
1 tablespoon plus 1½ teaspoons sugar
½ cup neutral-flavored cooking oil, such as canola or soybean

Whisk together the vinegar, lemon juice, salt, black pepper, basil, sugar, and oil.

MAKE AHEAD The vinaigrette will keep for up to 7 days in the refrigerator.

BREADED HALIBUT CHEEKS

SERVES 4

IN THE PACIFIC NORTHWEST, halibut season begins in March and lasts until late summer, but halibut cheeks are a delicacy with which few people are familiar. Halibut cheeks have a distinctive texture, almost like a scallop, and they're more forgiving than the fillets or steaks in terms of cooking time. While other cuts are easily overcooked, halibut cheeks still taste delicious with a few extra minutes of cooking time. Although halibut cheeks can be found in most fish shops and in the frozen food sections of many grocery stores nationwide, if you can't find them, substitute halibut fillets cut into 3-ounce pieces. Halibut cheeks vary greatly in size; the smaller ones have more flavor. Serve three small cheeks per person. Adjust accordingly if you're using larger cheeks.

2 cups fresh bread crumbs

4 ounces Parmesan or other hard cheese (page 23), shredded (1 cup)

1 tablespoon chopped fresh flat-leaf parsley

$3/4$ teaspoon garlic powder

$1/4$ teaspoon chili powder

1 teaspoon kosher salt

$1/2$ teaspoon freshly ground black pepper

$1/4$ cup extra-virgin olive oil

$3/4$ cup all-purpose flour

2 large eggs, beaten

$1/3$ cup milk

8 to 12 halibut cheeks or 2 pounds skinless halibut fillets, cut on the bias into 8 pieces

Preheat the oven to 450°F.

Put the bread crumbs, cheese, parsley, garlic powder, chili powder, salt, and pepper in a food processor. With the processor running, drizzle in the olive oil. Process until the bread crumbs are coated in the oil, about 15 seconds.

In three separate bowls, place the bread crumb mixture, flour, and eggs. Add the milk to the eggs and whisk to combine.

Put a baking sheet in the oven for 5 minutes. Dredge 1 halibut cheek in the flour and shake off any excess. Then dip the cheek in the eggs and then in the bread crumbs, pressing the bread crumbs lightly to coat the flesh evenly. Repeat the process with each piece of fish. Remove the pan from the oven and place the pieces on the hot baking sheet.

Bake the cheeks for 8 to 10 minutes, or until the bread crumb coating is golden brown and a meat thermometer inserted in the thickest part of the halibut reads 140°F. If additional cooking time is needed, continue to bake the fish, checking the temperature at 2-minute intervals. If you have a convection oven, turn it on for this recipe, as it makes the cheeks a beautiful brown color, but reduce the cooking time to 5 or 6 minutes total.

Serve immediately.

THE FISH DEBATE: FARMED OR WILD?

We're used to cows, pigs, and chickens coming from farms, but fish? Fish farming, also known as aquaculture, does have some benefits, but questionable nutritional and environmental consequences occur as well.

Fish farms produce almost 20 percent of all seafood globally. Seafood such as catfish, tilapia, trout, shrimp, mussels, and salmon are widely farmed. The majority of fish farms are in Asia, China in particular, but Norway and Chile control the farmed salmon trade, producing about 1 million tons of farmed salmon in 2004. In the United States, 30 percent of all seafood consumed comes from fish farms.

Fish farmers use several methods. Tuna and salmon are usually raised in open net pens and cages in coastal areas or freshwater lakes. Catfish, tilapia, and shrimp are raised in ponds. Farmers grow shellfish, such as clams, oysters, and mussels, on beaches or suspended in water using ropes or mesh bags.

Farmed fish has become a significant food source because so many fish and shellfish species are overfished and the wild populations are declining; more than 70 percent of the world's fisheries are exploited or severely depleted, according to the nonprofit trade association Seafood Choices Alliance. So, on one hand, farmed fish offer an alternative to perpetuating this grim overfishing problem. But the primary concern about farmed fish is what the fish are fed. Natural and artificial additives are fed to farmed fish to give it a more appealing color, while polychlorinated biphenyls (PCBs), dioxins, banned pesticides, and fungicides have also been found in their feed. PCBs are highly toxic industrial compounds that have been found in fishmeal and fish oil manufactured from small, open-sea fish. Numerous studies have shown that PCBs cause cancer in rats and have effects on human reproductive, immune, and neurological systems. They were banned from production in the United States in 1977, but they still exist in the sediment of some streams and rivers and in the flesh of fish.

Nutritional differences between wild and farmed fish have also been found. Nutrition expert Dr. Andrew Weil and the *American Journal of Clinical Nutrition,* as well as the USDA, found that farmed salmon has lower levels of omega-3s than wild salmon, and a higher fat content (11 to 20 percent for the farmed salmon versus 7 percent for the wild salmon). Omega-3s, which are fatty acids found in seafood, have been found to lower cholesterol levels and help prevent certain types of cancer.

The environmental impact of farmed fish is also high: The concentration of fish spreads disease more rapidly, and the entire ecosystem is affected when fish escape and breed with wild fish. Another concern is an increase in pollutants in the water where the fish are raised, especially from the high dose of antibiotics that drift from the pens.

In both wild and farmed fish, mercury levels have recently become a concern. Mercury can come from both natural and man-made sources, and exposure to high levels can lead to loss of short-term memory, motor skill impairment, and learning disabilities, and it can damage fetuses. According to the FDA, the Environmental Protection Agency (EPA), and numerous health and environmental groups, canned tuna, swordfish, shark, tilefish, and king mackerel contain the highest levels of mercury.

The right answer isn't clear, but aquaculture is here to stay as demand for seafood grows. Beyond the distinction between wild and farmed, elements to consider are flavor, business practices, and nutrition. Some farmed seafood is delicious, such as mussels, but I suspect I will always find the taste of local wild salmon far superior to that of farmed salmon.

For more information, go online to Seafood Choices Alliance (*www.seafoodchoices.org*), a nonprofit global trade association established to look at the issue of ocean-friendly seafood. The alliance works with fishermen, fish farmers, distributors, wholesalers, retailers, restaurants, and chefs to promote sustainable seafood sources.

POULTRY & MEAT

TURKEY JOES

TURKEY MEATLOAF STUDDED WITH CHEESE CURDS

CITRUS-HERB-MARINATED TURKEY TENDERLOINS

RACLETTINE

LEMON-HARISSA CHICKEN

CITRUS-GRILLED CHICKEN

KALE-STUFFED CHICKEN BREASTS

APRICOT-DIJON-GLAZED PORK TENDERLOIN

MEXICAN-STYLE SEASONED PORK

GRILLED PORK BLADE STEAKS

PORK CHOPS WITH MARMALADE SAUCE

LAMB STEW WITH RED WINE AND MUSHROOMS

SLOW-COOKED ORANGE-CHILI PORK SHOULDER

BEEF TENDERLOIN MEDALLIONS WITH RED WINE REDUCTION

GRILLED NEW YORK STEAK WITH BALSAMIC-MUSHROOM RAGOUT

TURKEY JOES

SLOPPY JOES, THE OLD CHILDHOOD FAVORITE, get a makeover in this weeknight dish. With turkey instead of beef and the addition of corn, cilantro, and jalapeño, this is no ordinary joe. Spoon this flavorful mixture into hamburger buns or warm tortillas for a kid-friendly main course, or try it over rice or in a lettuce cup.

1 pound ground turkey

$1\frac{1}{2}$ teaspoons kosher salt, or more to taste

1 garlic clove, minced

2 tablespoons neutral-flavored cooking oil, such as canola or soybean

1 medium yellow onion, diced

$\frac{1}{2}$ red bell pepper, diced

1 jalapeño pepper, seeded and minced

1 teaspoon ground cumin

$\frac{3}{4}$ teaspoon chili powder

$1\frac{3}{4}$ cups Chicken Stock (page 230) or store-bought low-sodium chicken broth

2 tablespoons tomato paste

1 large ear yellow corn, kernels removed (about $\frac{2}{3}$ cup), or $\frac{2}{3}$ cup frozen, defrosted

2 plum tomatoes, diced

$\frac{1}{4}$ cup chopped fresh cilantro

Freshly ground black pepper

In a medium bowl, combine the turkey, 1 teaspoon of the salt, and the garlic. Mix thoroughly.

In a large, dry skillet over high heat, sear the turkey mixture for 2 to 3 minutes on one side before stirring and breaking it apart with a spatula. Continue cooking the turkey for 5 to 7 minutes over medium heat, or until golden brown. Transfer the turkey to a bowl.

Heat the oil in the skillet and add the onion and bell pepper. Cook for 2 minutes, stirring occasionally. Add the jalapeño, cumin, chili powder, and remaining $\frac{1}{2}$ teaspoon salt. Cook and stir for 1 minute. Stir in the stock and tomato paste and return the turkey to the pan. Bring the mixture to a boil and cook for 5 minutes, or until the liquid is reduced by half. Remove from the heat. Stir in the corn, tomatoes, and cilantro. Taste for seasoning and add salt and pepper as needed. Serve hot.

MAKE AHEAD This is a great make-ahead dish; cover and refrigerate the cooked turkey mixture for up to 5 days. Reheat in a saucepan on low heat.

TURKEY MEATLOAF
Studded with Cheese Curds

SERVES 6

THIS MEATLOAF IS DRESSED-UP COMFORT FOOD. Made with ground turkey, chicken sausage, and cheese curds, it's a healthy dish that might just replace your mom's recipe as the best meatloaf around. You can use any cheese, but we like using curds because they don't melt completely, adding texture in every bite, while the cheese curds on the outside of the meatloaf get deliciously caramelized. The leftovers make terrific meatloaf sandwiches.

1½ pounds ground turkey

4 ounces Italian chicken or pork sausage, casings removed

5 ounces fresh cheese curds, roughly chopped, or Monterey Jack cheese, cut into ¼-inch pieces (1 cup)

½ medium yellow onion, minced

½ stalk celery, minced

2 garlic cloves, minced

2¼ teaspoons House Herbs (page 233) or other Italian herb blend

1 teaspoon kosher salt

½ teaspoon freshly ground black pepper

⅛ teaspoon cayenne pepper

1½ cups fresh bread crumbs

Preheat the oven to 350°F. Lightly oil a rimmed baking sheet or loaf pan.

In a large bowl, combine the turkey and sausage and mix thoroughly.

In a medium bowl, combine the cheese, onion, celery, garlic, herbs, salt, black pepper, cayenne, bread crumbs, and 6 tablespoons water, mixing gently. Add the cheese mixture to the meat mixture and combine gently. Do not overmix.

Form the meat mixture into a loaf that is uniform in thickness, approximately 2½ to 3 inches high and 8 inches long, and place it on the prepared baking sheet or loaf pan. Moisten your hands with a little water and pat down the loaf to form a smooth surface.

Bake for 45 to 55 minutes, or until golden brown and a meat thermometer inserted into the center of the meatloaf registers 160°F. Let the meatloaf rest for 10 minutes before serving.

MAKE AHEAD The baked meatloaf will keep, covered, in the refrigerator for up to 5 days.

CITRUS-HERB-MARINATED TURKEY TENDERLOINS

SERVES 4

WHILE MOST PEOPLE KNOW TURKEY ONLY as sliced cold cuts or a whole roasted bird for Thanksgiving dinner, turkey tenderloins are a versatile, tender cut. The citrus-herb marinade is crucial to both the flavor and the texture of the dish because it helps tenderize the meat and boosts the flavor. Serve this dish with Sausage-Oyster Stuffing, Wild Mushroom Stuffing, or Apple-Pecan Stuffing with Dried Cherries (pages 167–71), and you can enjoy the flavors of Thanksgiving all year long.

$^2/_3$ cup plus 3 tablespoons extra-virgin olive oil

$^1/_4$ cup capers, drained and mashed

6 garlic cloves, minced

$^1/_3$ cup freshly squeezed lemon juice (1 to 2 lemons)

2 tablespoons fresh thyme

1 tablespoon chopped fresh rosemary

1 tablespoon chopped fresh sage

$^1/_4$ teaspoon paprika

$1^3/_4$ teaspoons kosher salt

2 teaspoons freshly ground black pepper

2 pounds turkey tenderloins

Combine $^2/_3$ cup of the olive oil and the capers, garlic, lemon juice, thyme, rosemary, sage, paprika, salt, and pepper in a small bowl.

Tenderize both sides of the turkey tenderloins with a fork, piercing the meat all the way through about 10 times per side. Place the turkey in a large resealable plastic bag or a large bowl and add the marinade. Make sure the turkey is coated on all sides. Marinate in the refrigerator for at least 1 hour and up to 3 hours.

In a large skillet, heat the remaining 3 tablespoons oil over medium-high heat. Carefully add the turkey tenderloins and cook for 4 minutes, or until brown. (The oil may splatter when you add the turkey to the skillet.) Flip the turkey and cook for another 4 minutes. Reduce the heat to medium-low, flip the turkey again, and cook, covered, for 5 to 8 minutes, until a meat thermometer inserted in the thickest part of the turkey reads 140°F. Serve hot.

MAKE AHEAD The cooked turkey may be refrigerated for up to 3 days. Allow it to return to room temperature before serving or reheating it, covered, for 15 minutes in a 400°F. oven. Uncover and continue baking for an additional 5 to 10 minutes before serving.

NATURAL FOODS: A PRIMER

Besides seeking fresh ingredients and buying locally, avoiding additives and preservatives is important in the quest for pure flavor. Not only do these ingredients compromise the real flavor of natural foods, they are often unnecessary and of questionable nutritive value—even, in extreme cases, potentially harmful to your health. Here are definitions of common terms you may come across when shopping for food.

NATURAL: This government-regulated term indicates that the food comes from a plant or mineral source that has not been altered except by chopping, grinding, separating, drying, freezing, heating, or fermenting, and that the food contains no chemical additives (including colorings) or preservatives. For meats and poultry, the term *natural* means minimally processed and free of artificial products (such as coloring and nitrite). *Natural* does not necessarily cover hormone use, organic feed, or other environmental practices.

ORGANIC: This government-regulated term means the food was grown or raised under an ecological management system that generally rejects synthetic fertilizers and pesticides and promotes practices that restore, maintain, and enhance ecological harmony. The farm is required by the Organic Food Production Act and National Organic Program (NOP), part of the USDA, to meet organic standards and receive mandatory certification of organic production. Recent relaxing of government rules may be weakening the value of this designation, however; organic food can still contain preservatives and artificial additives, so read labels carefully.

WHOLE FOODS: While not a government-regulated term, *whole foods* is used often in discussions about food and by some food producers. It refers to food that is as near its original form as possible. It is generally the least processed version of any food in a given category, including grains, beans, fruits, and vegetables. Many people believe these foods retain greater natural nutritional value than foods that have been heavily processed or refined, even though vitamins and minerals may have been added to the formula after processing.

FOOD ADDITIVES: Food additives are chemicals, both of natural and artificial origin, that are added to foods, beverages, pharmaceuticals, and other products either to prolong their shelf life or change their flavor, odor, or appearance. Although people have been chemically preserving foods for thousands of years, the last few decades have brought a dramatic rise in the variety and prevalence of these controversial substances. Studies about the effects of food additives began in the last fifty years, and additives are regulated by the FDA. They generally fall into three categories: preservatives, flavor enhancers, and coloring agents.

Preservatives: Added to products to prevent spoilage or physical or chemical changes that affect color, flavor, texture, or appearance. Hydrogenated oils, also known as trans fats or trans fatty acids, along with sodium benzoate and sulfur dioxide, are a few examples of commonly used preservatives.

Flavor enhancers: Added to food to heighten flavor or to replace flavor lost during processing, or, in the case of sugar substitutes, to achieve a low-calorie product that tastes sweet. High fructose corn syrup, aspartame, artificial flavors, sucralose, MSG, and hydrolyzed proteins are common flavor enhancers.

Coloring agents: Used extensively in processed food to improve appearance. Foods with labels that say "artificial colors" use coloring agents; nitrates and nitrites are other common coloring agents.

RACLETTINE

THIS RECIPE WAS INSPIRED BY TWO DISHES: the French-Canadian poutine and the Swiss raclette. Poutine is a popular dish comprising French fries, gravy, and cheese curds that is sold on the streets of Quebec and in the finest restaurants of Montreal. Raclette is both a hard French cow's-milk cheese and a Swiss dish prepared by melting thin slices of cheese over broiled potatoes, pickles, and sausage. Our version combines the best of both, with meat, potatoes, green beans, and cheese in one hearty winter dish. Chicken rosemary sausage gives the most flavor to this dish, but pork sausage will work just as well.

1/2 tablespoon unsalted butter

1 pound chicken or pork sausage, casings removed

1 cup red wine

2 large Yukon Gold potatoes, cut lengthwise into 3/4-inch-wide pieces (about 1 1/4 pounds)

Kosher salt and freshly ground black pepper to taste

6 ounces green beans, cut into 2-inch pieces

1/2 medium red onion, thinly sliced

1 teaspoon extra-virgin olive oil

8 ounces fresh mozzarella, roughly chopped (2 cups)

Chicken Gravy (recipe follows)

8 to 10 cornichons, roughly chopped (see Note)

4 marinated artichoke hearts, drained and roughly chopped

1 teaspoon fresh thyme

In a medium skillet over medium heat, melt the butter. Add the sausage and cook, stirring occasionally, until lightly browned, about 5 minutes. Add the wine and cook for 12 to 15 minutes, or until the liquid is evaporated and the sausage browned. Set aside.

Center a rack in the oven and preheat to 425°F. Set up a large steamer on the stove.

Toss the potatoes with salt and pepper and steam them for 10 minutes. Add the green beans and steam for 5 more minutes.

While the potatoes and green beans are steaming, prepare the onions. In a medium bowl, toss the onions with the olive oil and salt and pepper. Pour the onions into an 8-inch baking dish. Bake for 20 minutes until softened and beginning to brown, and then transfer the onions to a separate bowl; reserve the baking dish.

Preheat the broiler.

Pour the potatoes and green beans into the baking dish. Layer the onion, sausage, and cheese on top of the potatoes. Broil for 3 minutes, until the cheese is melted and browned.

Top the dish with the gravy, cornichons, artichoke hearts, and thyme. Serve warm.

NOTE Cornichons are available at most grocery stores. If you can't find them, you can substitute about 1/3 cup chopped dill pickles.

Chicken Gravy

MAKES 1¹/₃ CUPS

Serve this flavorful gravy over any poultry dish or Turkey Meatloaf (page 111).

2 cups Chicken Stock (page 230) or store-bought low-sodium chicken broth

1 large sprig fresh thyme

1 tablespoon diced red onion

2 tablespoons all-purpose flour

¹/₂ cup milk

2 teaspoons soy sauce

Kosher salt and freshly ground black pepper to taste

In a medium skillet over high heat, combine the chicken stock and thyme and bring to a boil. Cook for 10 minutes, or until the liquid is reduced by half. Remove the thyme and add the red onion. Cook for 3 minutes, and then reduce the heat to low.

In a small bowl, make a slurry by combining the flour and milk. Slowly add the slurry to the reduced stock, whisking to combine. Cook for 2 minutes, and then stir in the soy sauce. Taste for seasoning; add salt and pepper as needed. Serve hot.

MAKE AHEAD The gravy will keep, covered, in the refrigerator for up to 5 days. Reheat gently over medium heat before serving.

LEMON-HARISSA CHICKEN

SERVES 6

HARISSA IS A FIERY MOROCCAN SPICE BLEND made with chili peppers that appears often in Mediterranean cooking. It comes both dried and as a paste, and when we started selling the spice at Pasta & Co we created this dish to celebrate its vibrant flavor. The trick here is pounding the chicken breasts until they are uniformly thin to let the marinade penetrate, which both flavors and tenderizes the meat.

2/3 cup extra-virgin olive oil

1/4 cup capers, drained and smashed

6 garlic cloves, minced

1/3 cup freshly squeezed lemon juice
    (1 to 2 lemons)

3 tablespoons minced fresh rosemary

2 tablespoons paprika

1 tablespoon harissa

1 3/4 teaspoons kosher salt

2 teaspoons freshly ground black pepper

6 boneless, skinless chicken breast halves
    (3 1/2 pounds)

2 1/2 tablespoons all-purpose flour

To make the marinade, in a small bowl, combine the olive oil, capers, garlic, lemon juice, rosemary, paprika, harissa, salt, and pepper.

Pound the chicken breasts one by one to an even 1/2-inch thickness between 2 sheets of waxed paper, using a meat tenderizer or the bottom of a heavy, flat-bottomed pan.

Place the chicken in a large resealable plastic bag or a large bowl and add the marinade. Make sure the chicken is coated on all sides and refrigerate it for at least 3 hours and up to 6 hours.

Prepare your grill by scraping it, oiling it, and heating it to high heat.

Remove the chicken from the marinade, reserving the liquid. Place the chicken breasts a few inches apart on the grill. If you are using a charcoal grill, place the chicken on the grill directly over the hot coals. Grill the chicken for 4 to 6 minutes on each side, or until cooked through (the chicken should be 165°F. in the center when tested with a thermometer). Cover with aluminum foil while you prepare the sauce.

To make the sauce, combine the remaining marinade with 2 1/2 cups water in a medium saucepan. Bring to a boil on high heat and cook for 1 1/2 minutes. Whisk the flour into 1/3 cup cool water and add to the marinade, stirring constantly. Bring to a boil to thicken the sauce slightly. Remove from the heat and cool slightly.

Pour the sauce over the chicken and serve.

MAKE AHEAD The chicken tastes best freshly grilled, but the cooked chicken will keep in the refrigerator for up to 2 days. Reheat in the oven, wrapped in foil, at 375°F. for 25 minutes.

CITRUS-GRILLED CHICKEN

SERVES 4

THIS RECIPE IS AKIN TO A HOMEMADE ROTISSERIE CHICKEN without the hassle. Use the lime marinade below as a base recipe; feel free to add more fresh herbs, other citrus fruit, shallots, or ginger.

½ cup extra-virgin olive oil

⅓ cup freshly squeezed lime juice (about 2 limes)

6 garlic cloves, roughly chopped

1 tablespoon chopped fresh flat-leaf parsley

1½ teaspoons packed light brown sugar

2 teaspoons kosher salt

¼ teaspoon freshly ground black pepper

Pinch of cayenne pepper

1 whole chicken (about 4 pounds), halved

To make the marinade, in a small bowl, combine the olive oil, lime juice, garlic, parsley, brown sugar, salt, black pepper, and cayenne and stir. Place the chicken in a large resealable plastic bag or a large bowl and add the marinade. Make sure the chicken is coated on all sides and refrigerate it for at least 1 hour and up to 3 hours.

While the chicken is marinating, prepare the grill by scraping it, oiling it, and heating it to low heat. If you are using a charcoal grill, spread the hot coals around the outside edges of the grill, making enough space so the chicken can sit on the cooking grate with no coals directly under it. Lay the chicken on the grill and cook for about 1 hour, flipping the chicken every 10 to 15 minutes, until it is cooked through (the chicken should be 165°F. in the leg when tested with a thermometer). If using a charcoal grill, you will need to replenish the hot coals every half hour or so. Let the chicken rest for 5 to 10 minutes before serving.

MAKE AHEAD To keep leftover chicken, remove the meat from the bones, discard the bones, and refrigerate the chicken in a covered container for up to 5 days.

BALSAMIC AND FRESH THYME–GRILLED CHICKEN

Prepare Citrus-Grilled Chicken, adding 2 tablespoons balsamic vinegar and 2 teaspoons fresh thyme to the marinade.

SPICY CHILE–GRILLED CHICKEN

Prepare Citrus-Grilled Chicken, adding 2 teaspoons ground cumin, 1 teaspoon chili powder, ½ teaspoon cayenne pepper, and 1 teaspoon dried oregano to the marinade.

KALE-STUFFED CHICKEN BREASTS

SERVES 6

STUFFED CHICKEN BREASTS ARE EASY TO PREPARE but have a wow factor that will impress your guests (or your family). Earthy kale and savory olive tapenade come together to dress up ordinary chicken.

3 large boneless, skinless whole chicken breasts (about 2½ pounds)

Kale and Tapenade Stuffing (recipe follows)

4 cups fresh bread crumbs

1½ ounces semihard cheese (page 23), shredded (6 tablespoons)

2 tablespoons chopped fresh flat-leaf parsley

¾ teaspoon kosher salt

¾ teaspoon freshly ground black pepper

¼ cup extra-virgin olive oil

¼ teaspoon Tabasco or other hot sauce

¾ cup all-purpose flour

2 large eggs

¾ cup milk

Cut each whole chicken breast into two halves, following the line that separates the two sides. Trim the breasts of fat and cartilage. Using a sharp knife, make a deep pocket in each half of the chicken breast by slicing it horizontally from the thick end to the thin end on the underside of the breast. Do not cut all the way through to the other side.

Divide the stuffing into 6 equal portions, about ⅓ cup each. Fill each pocket with the stuffing. Press the edges of the chicken together, securing the filling inside the chicken. Do not flatten the breast. Refrigerate the stuffed breasts until you are ready to bread and bake them.

Position a rack at the top of the oven and preheat the oven to 450°F.

Combine the bread crumbs, cheese, parsley, and ½ teaspoon each of the salt and pepper in a food processor or by hand; be sure the bread crumbs are finely ground. With the processor running, drizzle in the olive oil and hot sauce. Process until the bread crumbs are coated in the oil, about 15 seconds.

In three separate bowls, place the bread crumb mixture, flour, and egg. Add the milk to the egg and whisk to combine. Add the remaining ¼ teaspoon salt and ¼ teaspoon pepper to the flour and mix well.

Place a rimmed baking sheet in the oven for 5 minutes.

Dredge one stuffed chicken breast in the flour and shake off any excess. Coat the chicken in the egg and then the bread crumbs, pressing the bread crumbs lightly to coat the breast evenly. Repeat the process with each piece. Remove the pan from the oven and place the chicken pieces on the hot pan.

Bake for 25 to 30 minutes, or until the bread crumb coating is golden brown and a meat thermometer inserted in the thickest part of the chicken reads 165°F. (Be sure to test the temperature of the chicken meat and not the stuffing.) If you have a convection oven, turn it on for this recipe, as it turns the chicken breasts a beautiful brown color, but reduce the cooking time to 20 minutes.

Serve the chicken breasts immediately, cut into thick slices, or let them cool and serve at room temperature.

MAKE AHEAD The cooked chicken breasts may be refrigerated for up to 3 days. Allow them to return to room temperature before serving or reheating them, covered, for 15 minutes in a 400°F. oven. Uncover and continue baking for an additional 5 to 10 minutes before serving.

Kale and Tapenade Stuffing

MAKES ABOUT 2 CUPS

While it's great for chicken, this stuffing is also delicious on toast and as a sandwich spread.

1/4 cup extra-virgin olive oil	6 ounces fromage blanc or cream cheese
4 large shallots, chopped	(3/4 cup)
4 cups tightly packed chopped kale leaves	4 ounces semihard cheese (page 23),
1/3 teaspoon kosher salt	grated (3/4 cup)
1/3 teaspoon freshly ground black pepper	3 tablespoons olive tapenade

In a medium saucepan, heat the olive oil over medium-low heat. Add the shallots and sauté for 1 minute. Add the kale, salt, and pepper and sauté for 2 minutes, or until the kale is softened. Remove the kale from the heat, add the cheeses and tapenade, and gently combine. Refrigerate the stuffing for at least 1 hour and up to 3 days.

MAKE AHEAD The chicken breasts can be stuffed and refrigerated 1 day before breading and baking them.

APRICOT-DIJON-GLAZED
PORK TENDERLOIN

SERVES 4 TO 6

BECAUSE FRUIT, VINEGAR, AND MEAT HAVE A NATURAL AFFINITY, this recipe pairs apricot preserves and Dijon mustard to turn an ordinary pork tenderloin into an impressive main course. Served with Three-Grain Risotto (page 65), it makes an easy yet elegant meal.

2 medium yellow onions, thinly sliced

4 teaspoons extra-virgin olive oil

2 pounds pork tenderloin

2 teaspoons kosher salt

Freshly ground black pepper to taste

Apricot-Dijon Glaze (recipe follows)

1 cup Chicken Stock (page 230) or store-bought low-sodium chicken broth

Preheat the oven to 400°F.

Toss the onions with the olive oil and pour them into a 9 x 13-inch baking dish. Bake for 20 minutes.

While the onions are baking, season the pork with the salt and pepper.

Set the seasoned pork on top of the onions and cover the pork with the glaze. Pour the stock around the pork.

Bake for 20 to 30 minutes, or until the pork reaches an internal temperature of 140°F. Remove from the oven and let the pork rest for 10 minutes before serving.

To serve, cut the pork into ½-inch to 1-inch slices and place 3 to 4 slices on each plate. Garnish with the onions and sauce from the bottom of the baking dish.

Apricot-Dijon Glaze

MAKES ABOUT 2/3 CUP

2/3 cup apricot preserves

2 tablespoons Dijon mustard

2 teaspoons whole-grain mustard

1/2 teaspoon kosher salt

1/4 teaspoon freshly ground black pepper

1/8 teaspoon cayenne pepper

In a small bowl, combine the preserves, Dijon mustard, whole-grain mustard, salt, black pepper, and cayenne.

MAKE AHEAD The glaze can be made up to 1 week ahead.

COOKING TEMPERATURES FOR PROTEINS

Cooking meat to specific temperatures is not only a food safety issue but also a flavor issue. The appearance, juiciness, flavor, and tenderness of meat are affected by the cooking temperature. Overcooked meat is tough and tasteless, while undercooked meat is not as tender or as flavorful as it could be.

Cooking meat to a specific temperature and testing it with a thermometer is the only way to ensure your protein is cooked perfectly without slicing open the food and letting the juices escape. Don't feel embarrassed about using a thermometer; even top chefs use instant-read thermometers.

The chart below lists two sets of temperatures. On one side you'll find my recommended temperatures, and on the other those recommended by the USDA. The temperatures I cook to may seem low, but that's because I like to let meat rest for 10 to 15 minutes before serving it. The meat increases in temperature by about 10 degrees during that resting time. Further, the juices in the meat redistribute instead of running out as you cut it.

If you do not follow the USDA-recommended temperatures, you subject yourself to a small risk of foodborne illness, but to me it's worth the risk because the flavor of meats cooked to these temperatures is far superior. (If you're cooking for the elderly or the very young, however, it's advisable to follow the government guidelines because those two groups are more at risk for illness than any other part of the population. Also, ground meat, especially hamburger meat, should always be fully cooked, as *E. Coli* is more of a problem wth ground meat than with whole pieces.)

The safe temperatures listed apply more to pork and poultry than any other protein because, in theory, they are more susceptible to the parasite called trichinosis, but the USDA applies those temperatures to all meat and poultry products. According to most butchers, trichinosis is destroyed when the pork temperature reaches 137°F., but according to the USDA the parasite is killed at 160°F. In reality, trichinosis has been almost entirely eliminated from pork in the United States, so it isn't the threat to health it once was. Salmonella, a bacteria often found in raw poultry and eggs, is killed at 165°F., according to the USDA.

	Recommended Cooking Temperature	USDA Recommended Cooking Temperature
CHICKEN	160°F.	165°F.
TURKEY	140°F.	165°F.
PORK	125°F. MEDIUM RARE 135°F. MEDIUM 150°F. PLUS, WELL DONE	160°F. MEDIUM 170°F. WELL DONE
BEEF AND LAMB	115°F. MEDIUM RARE 135°F. MEDIUM 150°F. PLUS, WELL DONE	150°F. MEDIUM RARE 160°F. MEDIUM 170°F. PLUS, WELL DONE

MEXICAN-STYLE SEASONED PORK

SERVES 4 TO 6

BONELESS PORK SIRLOIN is the natural choice for quick braising because it's leaner than pork shoulder and is thus a bit more tender, yet it still remains flavorful. In this recipe, the technique and the cut of meat allow you to achieve the richness of braised pork in much less time. This pork makes a great taco or burrito filling and can be the main ingredient in a taco salad. Squeeze a few limes wedges over the pork to brighten the flavors and add a handful of chopped fresh cilantro and a side of rice for a quick trip south of the border.

$2\frac{1}{4}$ pounds boneless pork sirloin chops, cut into $\frac{1}{2}$-inch cubes

1 teaspoon kosher salt

1 teaspoon freshly ground black pepper

2 tablespoons extra-virgin olive oil

1 cup Chicken Stock (page 230) or store-bought low-sodium chicken broth

1 7-ounce can or jar salsa verde (mild to medium)

6 large garlic cloves, roughly chopped

2 plum tomatoes, chopped

1 large yellow onion, chopped

$1\frac{1}{2}$ tablespoons ground cumin

1 tablespoon plus 1 teaspoon chili powder

1 tablespoon dried oregano

Dash of cayenne pepper

In a large bowl, season the pork with the salt and pepper.

In a 12-inch skillet over high heat, heat the oil and add the pork, searing it on one side until golden brown, about 5 minutes. Stir the pork and continue searing it on all sides for an additional 12 to 15 minutes, stirring occasionally. The pork is done when the liquid in the pan is evaporated and the meat is evenly browned on all sides.

Add the chicken stock, salsa verde, garlic, tomatoes, onion, cumin, chili powder, oregano, cayenne, and 3 cups water to the skillet. Bring to a simmer and cook for 30 to 45 minutes until the liquid is almost evaporated, stirring occasionally. Reduce the heat to medium and cook for about 5 minutes, or until the dish has the desired amount of sauce. The longer you cook it, the less sauce you will have. For more tender pork, add an additional $\frac{1}{2}$ cup water and continue cooking until the desired amount of sauce is reached.

MAKE AHEAD The pork can be prepared up to 5 days in advance or frozen for up to 3 months. Reheat, covered, in a saucepan over low heat.

GRILLED PORK BLADE STEAKS

SERVES 4

SO MANY FLAVORFUL CUTS OF PORK ARE AVAILABLE in grocery stores these days that it's worth looking beyond pork tenderloin and pork chops. Pork blade steaks are long, thin, bone-in steaks cut from the pork shoulder; they're an unusual cut, but available in most meat departments. Because the steaks can be tough, we created a marinade with a high acid content that breaks down the fibers in the pork, tenderizing the meat. Pork and chutney have a natural affinity, and we particularly like the sweet-hot flavor of Pasta & Co Roasted Tomato Chutney, but feel free to substitute your favorite brand.

½ cup extra-virgin olive oil
½ cup cider vinegar
4 garlic cloves, chopped
½ cup store-bought chutney

Kosher salt and freshly ground black
    pepper to taste
1 green onion (white and green parts),
    chopped
4 8-ounce pork blade steaks

Mix the oil, vinegar, garlic, chutney, 1 teaspoon salt, ½ teaspoon pepper, and green onion together in a small bowl. Place the steaks in a large resealable plastic bag or a large bowl and add the marinade. Make sure the steaks are coated on all sides. Marinate the steaks for 1 to 3 hours in the refrigerator. Take them out of the refrigerator 30 minutes prior to grilling, allowing them to reach room temperature.

Prepare the grill by scraping it, oiling it, and heating it to medium-high heat. Lay the steaks on the grill. After 4 minutes, flip the steaks and cook for another 3 minutes for medium.

COOKING WITH WINE

Wine is not only wonderful in the glass, it's also an important ingredient in cooking. Wine can add depth and complexity to a dish, assuming one heeds the old saying "Don't cook with a wine you wouldn't drink." That doesn't mean you need to spend a fortune on cooking wine, but it does mean that if a wine doesn't taste good to you on its own, it's not going to taste great in the final dish either. If you can afford to cook with the wine you're serving, that's a perfect flavor match.

When choosing a wine to cook with, think about how big a role the wine plays in the recipe. If you're making chicken braised in red wine or making a red wine reduction, pick a good-quality wine because it plays a key role in the dish. But if you're making fish stock you can use an everyday, inexpensive bottle of white wine. As a rule of thumb, white wines used for cooking should be light, fruity, and acidic (dry), and reds should be young and fruity; Sauvignon Blanc or Viognier are good choices if the recipe calls for a dry white wine, and for reds a good standby is any Rhône varietal, including Syrah. Rhône varietals have bright fruit flavors and are

light- to medium-bodied, and they're great choices for cooking because bringing a little fruit to a dish is the reason to cook with wine. Use a heavier-bodied red wine for heavier dishes such as beef and lighter-bodied reds for poultry dishes. Cooking with wine accentuates the flavors of the wine, so heavily oaked or highly tannic wines aren't good choices for cooking because once the wines are reduced, those oak and tannin elements can overwhelm the other flavors in the dish.

Try not to use that open half-bottle that has been in the refrigerator for a month. Open a fresh bottle—with the added benefit that you can have a glass while you cook. And whatever you do, stay away from bottles labeled "cooking wine"; they are usually cheap wines that food coloring, salt, and preservatives have been added to.

Many people wonder if the alcohol in wine burns off during cooking, and USDA research shows the following: If wine is added to a boiling liquid and then the dish is immediately removed from the heat, 85 percent of the alcohol remains; if the food is simmered with the wine for 15 minutes, 40 percent of the alcohol remains. After 2 hours of simmering, 10 percent of the alcohol remains. For flambés or flaming dishes, most, but not all, of the alcohol is burned off. Because wine contains only about 12 to 14 percent alcohol to begin with, this should be a minor concern for most people.

Sherry, Madeira, port, and Marsala are fortified wines that appear frequently in recipes. They add an intense flavor to a dish and stay fresh in your cupboard for months because of their higher alcohol content.

PORK CHOPS
with Marmalade Sauce

COOKING WITH MARMALADE is a great way to add a strong concentration of orange to a dish, and the high sugar content of the marmalade results in beautifully caramelized meat. We prefer to grill these pork chops, but you can pan-fry them as well.

3 tablespoons orange marmalade	5 tablespoons extra-virgin olive oil
1 tablespoon chili powder	6 garlic cloves, pressed
1 tablespoon kosher salt	4 10-ounce boneless pork chops (ask your
1 tablespoon freshly ground black pepper	butcher for thick-cut pork loin chops)
2 tablespoons cider vinegar	1 cup Chicken Stock (page 230) or
1 tablespoon whole-grain mustard	store-bought low-sodium chicken broth

To make the marinade, in a small bowl, combine the marmalade, chili powder, salt, pepper, vinegar, mustard, olive oil, and garlic.

Tenderize both sides of the pork with a fork, piercing the meat all the way through about 10 times per side. Place the pork in a large resealable plastic bag or a large bowl and add the marinade. Make sure the pork is coated on all sides. Refrigerate the pork for at least 3 hours and no more than 6 hours.

Remove the pork from the refrigerator 30 minutes prior to grilling.

Prepare your grill by scraping it, oiling it, and heating it to medium-high heat.

Remove the pork chops from the marinade, reserving the marinade, and lay them in the center of the grill. Grill for 3 minutes. Turn the pork chops 45 degrees and grill for another 3 minutes. Flip the pork chops and grill for 3 minutes before turning 45 degrees and cooking an additional 3 minutes for medium. A meat thermometer inserted in the thickest part of the meat should read 125°F.

Transfer the pork chops to a cutting board to rest while you make the sauce. Pour the reserved marinade into a medium skillet. Add the stock and bring to a boil. Boil for 3 minutes.

To serve, slice the pork into ½-inch-thick slices and drizzle the sauce on top.

LAMB STEW
with Red Wine and Mushrooms

SERVES 4 TO 6

THIS RICH LAMB STEW is perfect for cold winter nights. It leaves out the traditional potato in favor of mushrooms and oregano, which provide a wonderful earthy flavor. A final twist comes in the addition of soy sauce, which intensifies the taste of this satisfying dish.

2 pounds boneless leg of lamb, cut into 1 1/2-inch pieces

1 tablespoon plus 1 teaspoon dried oregano

3/4 teaspoon garlic powder

1 1/2 teaspoons kosher salt

1/2 teaspoon freshly ground black pepper

4 tablespoons extra-virgin olive oil

1 pound crimini mushrooms, stems removed

8 ounces whole cipolline or pearl onions, peeled

3 garlic cloves, minced

1 tablespoon minced fresh rosemary plus 1 teaspoon (optional)

1/4 cup soy sauce

3/4 cup red wine, such as Merlot

1 1/2 cups Chicken Stock (page 230) or store-bought low-sodium chicken broth

Preheat the oven to 350°F.

Season the lamb with 1 teaspoon of the oregano and the garlic powder, salt, and pepper.

Heat 2 tablespoons of the olive oil in a large Dutch oven or a heavy pot with a tight-fitting lid over medium-high heat. Brown the lamb in two batches until deeply browned on two sides (about 4 minutes per side). Remove the browned lamb to a large bowl.

Reduce the heat to medium heat. Add the remaining 2 tablespoons olive oil to the pot, along with the mushrooms and onions. Cover and cook for 3 minutes, stirring occasionally. Remove the onions from the pot and set aside. Add the remaining 1 tablespoon oregano, the garlic, and 1 tablespoon of the rosemary. Cook and stir for about 1 minute, being careful not to brown the garlic. Add the soy sauce, wine, and chicken stock. Stir to deglaze the bottom of the pot. Increase the heat to high, bring to a boil, and return the lamb and any accumulated juices to the pot. Remove the pot from the heat, cover with a tight-fitting lid, and place in the oven.

Bake for 1 hour, and then stir. Bake for an additional 45 minutes, remove from the oven, and test the lamb for tenderness by prodding it with a fork. If it is not tender, return it to the oven for 15 to 30 minutes. When the lamb is tender, add the reserved onions. Cover and return the pot to the oven and bake for 15 minutes.

Before serving, stir in the remaining 1 teaspoon rosemary. Serve hot.

MAKE AHEAD The stew can be refrigerated for 5 days or frozen for up to 3 months. Reheat in a covered saucepan over medium heat.

mushrooms

No other ingredient can lend that earthy, woodsy flavor mushrooms bring to a dish, and the fungi thrive in the rainy climate of the Pacific Northwest. Along with wild-caught salmon, mushrooms are one of the few foods you can forage for. (Just be sure you join an experienced forager, because there *are* some poisonous varieties.) Some of the best varieties resist cultivation, adding a bit of mystery to your dinner plate.

The familiar white cap mushroom and button mushrooms are the most common, but wild varieties have a captivating flavor. Bright orange chanterelle and dark black trumpets appear in the fall; scaly brown morels and exotic porcini show up in the spring. Saying the name of some mushrooms is almost as much fun as eating them: Reddish lobster mushrooms, with their soft texture and delicate flavor, are best when showcased in a pasta dish, and the sand-colored chicken of the woods have a remarkable textural resemblance to chicken when cooked. Brown-capped shiitakes are cultivated and available year-round, but their true season is spring and fall. Shiitakes are extremely versatile, and perfect for baking and sautéing. Remove the woody stems and use them to make a flavorful stock. Large, meaty portobellos, the grown-up version of the crimini mushroom, can be grilled or sautéed.

When choosing mushrooms, skip any that appear soggy or bruised. Store them in a brown paper bag in the refrigerator for up to 3 days. Never wash fresh mushrooms; simply brush off any dirt with a damp towel. Dried mushrooms will last for six months in an airtight container and can be reconstituted in any hot liquid, such as water or stock.

SLOW-COOKED ORANGE-CHILI PORK SHOULDER

SERVES 6

MAKE THIS RICH DISH ON A WINTER'S NIGHT, and for six hours your house will be filled with the wonderful aroma of slow-cooked pork. The longer and slower you cook it, the better it is. The pork has several layers of flavor, including deep orange from the fresh orange juice and marmalade, a kick from the chili powder, and a vinegar tang from the olives. Serve the pork as a pulled-pork sandwich, spooned over Parsnip-Herb Biscuits (page 247), over pasta, or with steamed potatoes.

3 tablespoons chili powder

1 tablespoon plus 1½ teaspoons kosher salt

1 tablespoon freshly ground black pepper

3 pounds boneless pork butt or shoulder roast

3 tablespoons extra-virgin olive oil

2 medium yellow onions, diced

12 garlic cloves, chopped

1 cup dry white wine

½ cup red wine vinegar

1 cup pitted green olives, roughly chopped

1 tablespoon fennel seeds

1 tablespoon grated orange zest

1 cup freshly squeezed orange juice (2 oranges)

3 tablespoons orange marmalade

3 to 4 cups Chicken Stock (page 230) or store-bought low-sodium chicken broth

In a small bowl, mix the chili powder and 1 tablespoon each of the salt and pepper. Rub the entire roast with the mixture, massaging it into the meat. Reserve any of the spices that don't stick to the roast.

Heat a large Dutch oven or a heavy pot with a tight-fitting lid over medium-high heat. Add 2 tablespoons of the olive oil. Place the pork in the pan and sear it on all sides until well browned but not burned, 10 to 15 minutes. Transfer to a plate; reserve the pot.

Heat the remaining 1 tablespoon olive oil in the pot, add the onions, and sauté, stirring frequently, until they are lightly browned and softened, about 4 minutes. Add the garlic and cook for 1 additional minute. Add the white wine and bring the mixture to a boil, scraping any browned bits off the bottom of the pan with a wooden spoon.

Add the vinegar, ½ cup of the olives, the fennel seeds, orange zest, orange juice, marmalade, remaining 1½ teaspoons salt, and any remaining spice rub, and stir. Return the pork to the pot. Add just enough chicken stock to come halfway up the roast, and bring the stock to a boil. Cover the pot and reduce the heat to low. Simmer gently for 1½ hours, adding more stock if necessary to maintain the level of the liquid. The pork is done when it pulls apart easily with a fork, approximately 3½ hours total. Add the remaining olives and remove from the heat.

If the pork was tied, remove the strings. Break the meat apart into small chunks using two forks.

Serve hot.

NOTE If you desire a thicker sauce, remove the pork from the liquid, set it aside, and cover it until ready to serve. Ladle about ¼ cup of the cooking liquid into a bowl, being careful to remove only the liquid. Add 1½ tablespoons all-purpose flour and whisk to combine. Pour the liquid back into the pan, whisking to combine. Increase the heat to bring the sauce to a boil. Boil the sauce until it thickens to a gravylike consistency, stirring frequently, about 5 minutes.

BEEF TENDERLOIN MEDALLIONS
with Red Wine Reduction

SERVES 4

CUT FROM THE SHORT LOIN SECTION, beef tenderloin is a succulent cut of meat. Grilling adds flavor, and with a sprinkling of dried herbs and an intense red wine sauce, the beef is even more flavorful.

2 pounds beef tenderloin

1 teaspoon garlic powder

1 teaspoon kosher salt

1 tablespoon freshly ground black pepper, plus more to taste

1 teaspoon House Herbs (page 233) or other Italian herb blend

1 tablespoon extra-virgin olive oil

Sea salt to taste

Red Wine Reduction (recipe follows)

Rub each side of the tenderloin with the garlic powder, kosher salt, pepper, and herbs. Set aside for 30 minutes. Just prior to grilling, drizzle the tenderloin all over with the olive oil, evenly coating it.

Preheat the oven to 400°F.

Prepare your grill by scraping it, oiling it, and heating it to high.

When the grill is as hot as possible, place the tenderloin in the center. If you are using a charcoal grill, place the tenderloin on the grill directly over the hot coals. Sear each side for 1 minute, moving the meat to a new spot on the grill each time you turn it. Cook each side of the tenderloin just long enough to sear it, not cook it through.

Remove the tenderloin from the grill and place it on a baking sheet. Roast it in the oven for 20 to 25 minutes for medium-rare. A meat thermometer inserted in the thickest part of the meat should read 115°F. Remove the meat from the oven, transfer it to a cutting board, and let it rest for 10 to 15 minutes before slicing.

To serve, slice the tenderloin into ½- to 1-inch medallions. Divide the medallions among 4 plates and sprinkle with sea salt and pepper. Drizzle the red wine reduction on top.

MAKE AHEAD The tenderloin can be seared on the grill several hours before cooking it. For dinner parties, sear the tenderloin before the party and then finish it in the oven.

Red Wine Reduction

MAKES ABOUT ½ CUP

This velvety sauce, made with a bottle of red wine and a bottle of port, a sweet fortified wine, enhances any meat it is served with. The wines are reduced with chicken stock for a sauce more intense than the average red wine sauce.

4 cups Chicken Stock (page 230) or store-bought low-sodium chicken broth
1 bottle (750 ml) red wine
1 bottle (750 ml) ruby port
1 sprig fresh thyme
1 sprig fresh rosemary
½ large yellow onion, quartered

1 carrot, roughly chopped
1 sweet apple, such as Fuji, cored and quartered
4 tablespoons (½ stick) unsalted butter
Kosher salt and freshly ground black pepper to taste
Pinch of sugar as needed

In a large saucepan, combine the chicken stock, wine, port, thyme, rosemary, onion, carrot, and apple. Bring to a boil, reduce the heat to low, and simmer for 30 minutes.

Strain the mixture, discarding the solids. Return the liquid to the pan, increase the heat to high, and boil for 30 minutes. Reduce the heat to medium-low and simmer until the liquid reduces to ½ cup, about 20 minutes. Watch the sauce carefully; it can burn if it is reduced too much.

Remove the pan from the heat. Add the butter and whisk until it is melted, about 1 minute. Taste and add salt and pepper as needed. If the sauce tastes sharp, add a pinch of sugar.

MAKE AHEAD The sauce will keep, covered, in the refrigerator for up to 5 days, or frozen for up to 6 months. Reheat it in a saucepan over low heat.

Véronique Drouhin

Maison Joseph Drouhin, the French wine estate known for its Burgundy wines, legitimized the Pacific Northwest wine scene when Robert Drouhin and his daughter Véronique arrived in Oregon in 1987 to establish Domaine Drouhin Oregon. Véronique Drouhin has overseen the groundbreaking venture, and her commitment to excellence and dedication to winemaking has made an unparalleled contribution to the wine culture of the Pacific Northwest.

Véronique began her journey from Beaune to Oregon's Willamette Valley in 1986 as an oenology student. Her father had visited the valley first in 1961, and when he returned in 1980, and after tasting Oregon wine, he saw the future of Pinot Noir in the Pacific Northwest. Robert Drouhin even arranged a blind tasting at his wine estate in Burgundy, where Oregon Pinot Noir held its own against top local wines. Mr. Drouhin entrusted Véronique with creating the new venture in 1987. "The winemakers in Oregon thought if people from Burgundy came, it would bring some respect to the area. That's how we started the adventure," Véronique says. "Originally we decided to make two vintages. Our decision was based on quality. If the wine was up to the standard we were looking for we would release it, but if we didn't think Oregon had a big future for Pinot we could just sell the land. Everyone was waiting to see what we made. We tried to stick to our rule: to produce a wine with finesse and complexity rather than power." Making wine from Pinot Noir grapes is challenging because it's a difficult grape to grow and the conditions have to be just right, but the Drouhins discovered the Oregon climate was perfect for the varietal. But respecting the differences between Oregon and Burgundy has been crucial. "The terroir is different, so we play with the differences and the similarities."

Domaine Drouhin produces 15,000 cases of Pinot Noir and Chardonnay annually. Besides her involvement in Oregon wine, Véronique has witnessed the change in the Pacific Northwest culinary scene as well. "There is fresh product everywhere, and high-quality food. The food has dramatically improved since I arrived," she says. "It used to be frustrating to not be able to find good cheese in Oregon, but now it's not a problem." Despite her commute from Oregon to Beaune, Véronique remains committed to Oregon because of the people. "I stay because of the people, the place, and the challenge also. You want to show people that what you believe in is worth it," she notes. "Burgundy is still home, but I have a strong commitment here. The people are wonderful and the community is wonderful. Everyone works together."

GRILLED NEW YORK STEAK
with Balsamic-Mushroom Ragout

SERVES 4

NEW YORK STEAK, also known as strip steak or shell steak, is a tender cut that comes alive on the grill. Mushrooms are the natural choice as a side dish, with balsamic vinegar adding a deep, sweet note to the earthy mushrooms.

1 teaspoon garlic powder
1 teaspoon kosher salt
1 tablespoon ground black pepper
2 1-pound New York steaks

1 tablespoon extra-virgin olive oil
Sea salt to taste
Balsamic-Mushroom Ragout (recipe
  follows)

In a small bowl, combine the garlic powder, salt, and pepper.

Sprinkle one-quarter of the rub on each side of the steaks, pressing firmly until it sticks. Drizzle the steaks with the oil and set aside for 30 minutes.

Prepare your grill by scraping it, oiling it, and heating it to medium-high.

When the grill is hot, lay the steaks in the center and grill them for 4 minutes without moving. Turn the steaks 45 degrees and grill for another 3 minutes. Flip the steaks and grill for 4 minutes, turn 45 degrees, and grill for an additional 3 minutes for rare. A meat thermometer inserted in the thickest part of the steaks should read 115°F.

Remove the steaks from the grill, transfer them to a cutting board, and let rest for 5 to 10 minutes. Cut each steak crosswise into ½-inch slices. Divide the meat among 4 plates, sprinkle with sea salt, and spoon the mushroom ragout on top.

Balsamic-Mushroom Ragout

MAKES ABOUT 1½ CUPS

Any type of mushroom can be used in the ragout, but we prefer crimini, which are flavorful, good sized, and reasonably priced. If you use portobello mushrooms, remove the black gills.

1 pound mushrooms, stems trimmed
¾ cup extra-virgin olive oil
1 tablespoon House Herbs (page 233) or other Italian herb blend

¾ cup chopped shallots
5 garlic cloves, chopped
½ cup balsamic vinegar
½ cup Worcestershire sauce

Cut the mushrooms into ¾-inch pieces.

Heat the oil in a large skillet over medium heat. Add the mushrooms, stir until they are fully coated, and sauté them for 3 minutes. Add the herbs, shallots, and garlic. Sauté for 2 more minutes, or until the mushrooms just begin to brown on the edges. Add the vinegar and Worcestershire sauce and reduce the heat to low. Simmer for 25 minutes, or until the sauce begins to look like a syrup. Remove from the heat.

MAKE AHEAD The ragout can be prepared in advance and refrigerated for up to 5 days. Reheat slowly over medium heat before serving.

certified organic
KOHLRABI
$1.75 bu.

VEGETABLES & SIDES

SUMMER VEGETABLE SAUTÉ

GRILLED ONION AND FENNEL RINGS

PAN-SEARED BROCCOLI CROWNS

PAN-ROASTED ORANGE-PAPRIKA CARROTS

BROILED SUNCHOKES

ROASTED AUTUMN VEGETABLES

BRUSSELS SPROUTS WITH GARLIC BREAD CRUMBS

RUSTIC BLUE CHEESE MASHED POTATOES

ROASTED PARSNIP PUREE

STUFFED PORTOBELLO MUSHROOMS

BRAISED KALE GRATIN

STUFFED MUSTARD GREENS

POTATOES AU GRATIN

RED, WHITE, AND GREEN VEGETABLE "LASAGNE"

LEMON-CAPER CAULIFLOWER

SAUSAGE-OYSTER STUFFING

WILD MUSHROOM STUFFING

APPLE-PECAN STUFFING WITH DRIED CHERRIES

SUMMER VEGETABLE SAUTÉ

SERVES 4 AS A SIDE DISH

WASHINGTON STATE CORN appears in markets in July and doesn't stop until September. Fresh, sweet corn is truly the taste of summer and takes only a few minutes to prepare. Vegetables are so plentiful in the summertime we always end up with bins of beans and corn, and after weeks of eating corn on the cob I came up with this simple way to celebrate the summer bounty.

1 tablespoon unsalted butter
$1/2$ medium yellow onion, diced
2 ears fresh yellow corn, kernels removed (about $1^1/3$ cups corn)

8 ounces green beans, cut into $3/4$-inch pieces
$1/2$ teaspoon kosher salt
$1/4$ teaspoon freshly ground black pepper
$1/8$ teaspoon garlic powder

In a medium skillet over medium heat, melt the butter. Add the onion and sauté for 4 minutes, stirring occasionally, until browned. Stir in the corn and cook for 2 minutes. Add the beans, salt, pepper, and garlic powder. Cook for 3 minutes, stirring occasionally, and remove from the heat.

Add 1 tablespoon water to the skillet and cover. Let the vegetables sit, covered, off the heat for 5 to 10 minutes before serving.

PIKE PLACE MARKET

Pike Place Market, Seattle's famous food market, is celebrating its centennial. In 1906, when the cost of onions skyrocketed, a Seattle councilman proposed a public street market where farmers could sell directly to the citizens. On August 17, 1907, Pike Place Market opened with eight farmers. Now it houses nearly 200 year-round commercial businesses, 190 craftspeople, and 120 farmers who rent table space by the day, as well as 240 street performers and musicians. It's the longest-running farmer's market in the country and host to more than 10 million visitors every year.

The market has quite a checkered history. In the 100 years of its existence, the market has had its ups and downs, and in the late 1960s the riptide of urban renewal nearly pulled it under. Local activist Victor Steinbrueck led the grassroots opposition to the developer's wrecking ball. A local historical district was created with a thick book of rules that keeps the market's ancient character but sometimes hampers its ability to move forward.

Locals call it "The Market," and newcomers are instantly identifiable when they refer to it as "Pike's Place Market" or "Pike's Market." The bounty varies with the season but is always inspiring: the crates of baby lettuce, the baskets of fresh figs, bushels of apples, bins of peaches, and unruly bunches of Chinese long beans. It's the only place in the world where you can find organic strawberries, grab a fresh croissant, buy a fillet of wild salmon, and get a tattoo all in one afternoon!

In the past ten years, farmer's markets have emerged as a major force in the local food scene all across America. In 2004 there were 3,700 farmer's markets in the United States, more than double the number from 1994, according to the USDA. A true farmer's market is the ultimate food experience—it's like visiting a farm without driving for hours to the countryside. Everything is fresh, you can talk to the people who grow the food, and you get only the best of what's in season. You won't find out-of-season tomatoes, that soulless fruit that lines the produce aisles in supermarkets. The seasonality of the market adds to the texture of life. Part of what makes those peak-of-the-season, bursting-with-flavor, juicy summer tomatoes so special is that you can't get them year-round. You have to wait for that time of year and then eat enough to hold you over until the following year. Think of music without rhythm—it's nothing. You need rhythm to keep things interesting, and farmer's markets keep the rhythm of the kitchen.

GRILLED ONION AND FENNEL RINGS

SERVES 4 TO 6 AS A SIDE DISH

IF YOU'VE GOT THE GRILL ON, nothing is easier than grilling sweet onions and fennel. Tossed with a balsamic dressing, the rich, caramelized flavors make a great side dish for meat, including Grilled New York Steak with Balsamic-Mushroom Ragout (page 136).

2 tablespoons extra-virgin olive oil
1 tablespoon balsamic vinegar
1¼ teaspoons kosher salt
½ teaspoon freshly ground black pepper
¼ teaspoon sugar

1 large red onion, sliced into ¼-inch-thick rings
1 large fennel bulb, green ends trimmed, woody parts discarded, cut into ¼-inch-thick rings

In a large bowl, whisk together the olive oil, vinegar, salt, pepper, and sugar. Add the onion and fennel and gently toss to coat the vegetables with the dressing.

Preheat an indoor grill or heat a large grill pan over medium-high heat. (A grill basket is ideal if you're using an outdoor grill.) Pour the vegetables onto the grill, spreading them out. Do not stir the vegetables for 2 minutes, allowing them to brown on one side. Using tongs, flip the vegetables and cook for an additional 2 minutes. Reduce the heat to low and let the vegetables cook for about 5 minutes, stirring occasionally, until browned and tender but not completely soft.

Remove the vegetables to a medium bowl and toss to separate. Serve warm.

PAN-SEARED BROCCOLI CROWNS

LET'S FACE IT: STEAMED BROCCOLI IS BORING, but pan-roasting broccoli in a dab of butter produces a vegetable even a kid would eat. To spice it up, I often throw in a mashed garlic clove and $\frac{1}{8}$ teaspoon red pepper flakes.

1 tablespoon unsalted butter

1 bunch broccoli, cut into medium florets

$\frac{1}{4}$ teaspoon kosher salt

$\frac{1}{4}$ teaspoon freshly ground black pepper

Heat a large skillet over high heat and melt the butter. Add the broccoli, salt, and pepper and stir until the butter is distributed evenly. Cook for 1 minute without stirring. Stir with a wooden spoon to turn the broccoli pieces and prevent them from burning. Cook the broccoli for 2 more minutes. Add 1 tablespoon water to the pan, remove the pan from the heat, cover, and set aside for 5 minutes to steam.

Serve warm.

PAN-ROASTED ORANGE-PAPRIKA CARROTS

SERVES 4 AS A SIDE DISH

THIS IS A TRIPLE-ORANGE VEGETABLE DISH: bright orange carrots, paprika, and orange juice come together to create a vibrant side dish.

- 1 tablespoon unsalted butter
- 3 large carrots, cut diagonally into ¼-inch-thick slices
- ¼ teaspoon kosher salt
- ¼ teaspoon freshly ground black pepper
- 2 tablespoons freshly squeezed orange juice
- ¼ teaspoon turbinado sugar or light brown sugar
- ¼ teaspoon paprika

Heat a large skillet over medium-high heat and melt the butter. Cook until the butter browns, about 3 minutes. Add the carrots and stir. Season with the salt and pepper and let brown for 2 minutes without stirring. Stir and let the carrots cook for an additional 2 minutes, or until they are just starting to soften.

Add the orange juice, sugar, and paprika and stir. Cook for 4 minutes, stirring occasionally, until the carrots have a brown glaze and are easily pierced with a fork. Turn off the heat, cover, and set aside until ready to serve. Serve warm.

MAKE AHEAD The carrots keep for up to 2 days in the refrigerator. Reheat them in a saucepan over low heat.

BROILED SUNCHOKES

SERVES 4 AS AN APPETIZER OR SIDE DISH

AFTER WALKING BY A BIN OF LOCALLY GROWN, knobby brown sunchokes one autumn afternoon, I became curious about this unusual ingredient. Also known as Jerusalem artichokes, they taste like a cross between an artichoke heart and a potato and are at their best in the fall and winter months. If you can't find sunchokes, substitute Yukon Gold potatoes.

4 tablespoons (1/2 stick) unsalted butter
1 pound sunchokes, unpeeled, cut into
    3/4-inch pieces
1/2 medium yellow onion, thinly sliced
2 large celery ribs, thinly sliced
1 tablespoon chopped, drained sun-dried
    tomatoes in oil
1 tablespoon ground green peppercorns

1/2 teaspoon kosher salt
1 tablespoon all-purpose flour
4 teaspoons pale dry sherry
2 tablespoons roughly chopped fresh
    flat-leaf parsley
4 ounces semihard cheese (page 23),
    grated (1 cup)

Preheat the broiler.

Heat a medium skillet on medium heat and melt the butter. Add the sunchokes and sauté for 10 minutes, or until brown. Add the onion and celery and sauté for 1 minute. Add the tomatoes, peppercorns, and salt. Sauté until the onions begin to caramelize, about 2 minutes. Add the flour and cook for 1 minute. Add the sherry and stir to deglaze the pan. Add the parsley and mix gently.

Transfer the sunchokes to a baking dish and top with the cheese. Broil for 3 minutes, or until the cheese is melted and beginning to brown. Serve hot.

Alex Golitzin

Washington wines are finally getting the respect they deserve, thanks to Alex Golitzin, owner of one of the state's premier wineries. Quilceda Creek Cabernet Sauvignon caught the attention of wine critic Robert Parker and has been named one of the best Cabernets in the United States—which is no surprise to us Pacific Northwest wine lovers.

Alex embodies the spirit of the Northwest. Down to earth, he makes his wines without flash or fanfare, despite his huge success. Instead, there is simply dedication and focus on producing excellent wine. Alex's reputation for making wines that age well while most other winemakers follow the trend of making wines that are instantly drinkable is an anomaly in this instant-gratification society. The winery is open only two days a year to mailing list customers, who pick up their wine and celebrate with a lunch cooked by Alex's wife, Jeannette.

Family tradition was partly responsible for bringing Alex into the wine business. He was a chemical engineer who wanted something more exciting. His uncle Andre Tchelistcheff, a major force in the American wine industry, made wine at Beaulieu Vineyards in California's Napa Valley, and then moved to Washington State to consult for Château Ste. Michelle. Alex moved to Washington in 1967, and in the mid-1970s Tchelistcheff urged him to make his own wine. Alex made one barrel of Cabernet Sauvignon every year until he released all 150 cases of his first wine in 1979. The 1979 Quilceda Creek went on to win a gold medal at a regional competition, and the rest is history.

According to Alex, what sets Washington State wine apart is the climate. "Eastern Washington is a wonderful place to grow Bordeaux varietals because we can get them really ripe," says Alex. "The thing that really has been successful for us is great vineyards. Without great vineyards, you can't make great wine."

His son Paul has joined the family tradition and now shares the winemaking duties. They make about 5,000 cases each year that immediately sell out to their mailing list and restaurant customers. These wines are a cult favorite that are well worth seeking out.

ROASTED AUTUMN VEGETABLES

SERVES 4

ROASTING VEGETABLES BRINGS OUT THEIR TRUE FLAVORS, and tossing them in a vinaigrette before roasting accentuates the flavors even more. Although red bell peppers are not an autumn vegetable, they add an undeniable flavor and color contrast to the other vegetables. Cut the vegetables into uniform pieces to ensure even cooking.

$\frac{1}{3}$ cup extra-virgin olive oil

2 garlic cloves, smashed and minced

1 teaspoon chopped fresh rosemary

$\frac{1}{2}$ teaspoon House Herbs (page 233) or other Italian herb blend

$1\frac{1}{4}$ teaspoons kosher salt

$\frac{1}{4}$ teaspoon freshly ground black pepper

1 medium butternut squash (about $1\frac{1}{2}$ pounds), peeled, seeded, and cut into $\frac{1}{2}$-inch pieces

1 red bell pepper, cut into $\frac{1}{2}$-inch pieces

1 medium yellow onion, cut into $\frac{1}{2}$-inch pieces

1 small celery root, peeled and cut into $\frac{1}{2}$-inch pieces

Preheat the oven to 400°F.

In a large bowl, combine the olive oil, garlic, rosemary, herbs, salt, and pepper. Add the squash, bell pepper, onion, and celery root. Toss until the vegetables are evenly coated in the dressing.

Pour the vegetables onto two baking sheets in a single layer.

Roast without stirring for 20 minutes. Rotate the pan and continue roasting for another 20 minutes, or until the vegetables are brown and easily pierced with a fork. Serve warm or at room temperature.

MAKE AHEAD This is a great make-ahead dish; the vegetables will keep for up to 5 days in the refrigerator. Reheat them, covered, in a 350°F. oven for 20 to 30 minutes.

BRUSSELS SPROUTS
with Garlic Bread Crumbs

SERVES 4 TO 6 AS A SIDE DISH

THE MUCH-MALIGNED BRUSSELS SPROUT can be the hit of the dinner table with just a few added ingredients. A sprinkling of garlic bread crumbs on top gives a nice crunch.

1¹⁄₃ cups cubed artisanal white bread

4 garlic cloves, minced

2 tablespoons extra-virgin olive oil

1 medium yellow onion, thinly sliced

¹⁄₄ teaspoon kosher salt

Freshly ground black pepper to taste

1¹⁄₂ pounds Brussels sprouts, stems and loose leaves trimmed, halved lengthwise

Preheat the oven to 325°F.

Lay the bread on a baking sheet and bake for 15 to 20 minutes, or until the cubes are toasted and golden. Using a food processor, pulse the bread and about one-third of the garlic until you have small pieces about the size of a lemon seed. Set aside.

In a medium skillet over medium-high heat, heat the olive oil. Cook the onion, stirring frequently, for 3 to 4 minutes, or until it begins to brown. Reduce the heat to medium, add the salt and pepper, and cook for 5 minutes, or until the onions are golden and are beginning to caramelize. Set aside.

Bring a large pot of salted water to a boil over high heat. Add the Brussels sprouts and the remaining garlic to the pot. Cook for 6 minutes, or until the Brussels sprouts are tender when pierced with a fork.

Drain the Brussels sprouts and place them in large bowl. Add the onions and toss. To serve, place the vegetables in a serving dish and sprinkle with the garlic bread crumbs. Serve warm or at room temperature.

MAKE AHEAD The Brussels sprouts will keep for up to 5 days in the refrigerator. Reheat them, covered, in a 350°F. oven for 20 to 30 minutes.

RUSTIC BLUE CHEESE
MASHED POTATOES

SERVES 4 AS A SIDE DISH

SMOKY BLUE CHEESE ADDS A DECISIVE TANG to ordinary mashed potatoes, and yams lend a great color and flavor. These creamy potatoes are a wonderful accompaniment to the Pan-Roasted Orange-Paprika Carrots (page 146) or virtually any meat dish in the book.

1 small yam, peeled and diced
1 tablespoon extra-virgin olive oil
2$\frac{1}{2}$ teaspoons kosher salt
$\frac{3}{4}$ teaspoon freshly ground black pepper
4 medium Yukon Gold potatoes (about 2 pounds)
$\frac{1}{2}$ cup milk

2 tablespoons unsalted butter, cut into $\frac{1}{2}$-inch pieces
2 ounces semihard cheese (page 23), grated ($\frac{1}{2}$ cup)
2 ounces smoky blue cheese (page 23), crumbled ($\frac{1}{2}$ cup)
$\frac{1}{2}$ teaspoon garlic powder
1 teaspoon minced fresh thyme

Preheat the oven to 400°F.

Place a baking sheet in the oven to heat for 5 minutes.

In a large bowl, toss together the yam dice, olive oil, 1 teaspoon of the salt, and $\frac{1}{2}$ teaspoon of the pepper. Pour onto the hot baking sheet. Bake for 20 minutes, or until the yams are brown and cooked through. Remove from the oven, transfer the yams to a medium bowl, and mash them. Set aside.

While the yams are roasting, peel half or all of the peel from the potatoes. (Leaving some of the peel on adds texture and color to the dish.) Cut the potatoes into 2-inch pieces. Put the potatoes in a large pot and cover them with cold water. Add 1 teaspoon of the salt, bring to a boil, and boil for 20 to 25 minutes, or until the potatoes are just cooked through.

In a small pot, heat the milk over low heat.

Strain the potatoes and return them to the pot. Add the butter, remaining salt and pepper, both cheeses, and the garlic powder, thyme, and warm milk. With a potato masher, gently mash the potato mixture. The potatoes should be slightly chunky.

Gently fold in the roasted yams with the masher or a spatula. Do not fully incorporate the yams; leave spikes of color throughout the potatoes. Serve warm.

MAKE AHEAD The potatoes will keep, covered, for up to 5 days in the refrigerator. Reheat, covered, in a 350°F. oven for 30 minutes. Add more milk if needed.

ROASTED PARSNIP PUREE

MAKES 3 CUPS

PARSNIPS HAVE NEVER CAUGHT ON IN THE UNITED STATES, but I love them for their earthy sweetness when roasted. A cousin of the carrot, parsnips are at their best in the fall and winter months. This puree is a great substitute for mashed potatoes and can be served alone or with additional ingredients, such as Roasted Butternut Squash and Fuji Apple (recipes follow), to create extra layers of flavor.

2 pounds parsnips, cut into $1/4$-inch pieces
   (about 6 to 8 parsnips)
1 tablespoon extra-virgin olive oil
$1/2$ teaspoon kosher salt
$1/4$ teaspoon freshly ground black pepper

1 cup milk
1 small clove garlic, chopped
2 ounces semihard cheese (page 23),
   grated ($1/2$ cup)

Preheat the oven to 500°F.

In a large bowl, toss the parsnips in the olive oil, salt, and pepper. Pour the parsnips onto a baking sheet and roast for 20 minutes, or until tender when pierced with a fork.

Using a food processor, pulse the milk and garlic together until the garlic is pureed. Add the roasted parsnips and cheese and pulse until smooth, just until the mixture comes together. Serve warm.

MAKE AHEAD The puree will keep, covered, for 5 days in the refrigerator. Reheat, covered, in a 350°F. oven for 20 to 30 minutes.

Roasted Butternut Squash

MAKES 4 CUPS

1 pound butternut squash, peeled, seeded, and roughly chopped

3 tablespoons extra-virgin olive oil

1 teaspoon kosher salt

½ teaspoon freshly ground black pepper

1 tablespoon fresh chopped rosemary, or 1 teapsoon dried

In a large bowl, toss squash with olive oil, salt, and pepper. Put the squash on a baking sheet next to the parsnips, keeping the two vegetables separate, and roast until tender and golden brown, 15 to 20 minutes.

Prepare the parsnip puree and transfer it to a separate bowl. Fold in the squash and the rosemary. Do not overmix. Taste for seasoning and stir in salt and pepper as needed.

Fuji Apple

MAKES 3 CUPS

1 pound Fuji apples (about 3 apples), peeled, cored, and chopped

2 tablespoons extra-virgin olive oil

½ teaspoon kosher salt

¼ teaspoon freshly ground black pepper

4 slices applewood-smoked bacon, cooked and crumbled

4 ounces blue cheese, crumbled (1 cup)

2 tablespoons chopped fresh thyme, or 2 teaspoons dried

Roast the parsnips for the parsnip puree and then lower the oven temperature to 425°F. In a medium bowl, toss apples with olive oil, salt, and pepper. Pour the apples onto a baking sheet and roast for 15 to 20 minutes, or until tender and easily pierced with a fork.

Prepare the parsnip puree, and add the apples, bacon, blue cheese, and thyme. Do not overmix. Taste for seasoning and add salt and pepper as needed.

STUFFED PORTOBELLO MUSHROOMS

SERVES 6

LARGE, MEATY PORTOBELLO MUSHROOMS were made for stuffing. This is a fabulous vegetarian entrée, with colorful vegetables and a creamy filling.

1/3 cup plus 3 tablespoons extra-virgin olive oil

Kosher salt and freshly ground black pepper

2 garlic cloves, minced

6 large mushrooms, such as portobellos, stems and gills removed, caps wiped clean

3 medium zucchini, diced

1 medium red bell pepper, sliced

1 large yellow onion, diced

3 ounces (6 tablespoons) cream cheese

3 tablespoons unsalted butter, softened

1 green onion (white and green parts), thinly sliced

1 ounce Parmesan or other hard cheese (page 23), grated (1/4 cup)

2 tablespoons sliced drained sun-dried tomatoes in oil

1 tablespoon chopped fresh basil

1 tablespoon chopped fresh flat-leaf parsley

2 tablespoons fresh bread crumbs

3 plum tomatoes, cut into 6 slices each

4 ounces semisoft cheese (page 23), grated (1 cup)

Preheat the oven to 400°F.

To cook the mushrooms, combine 1/3 cup of the olive oil, 1/2 teaspoon salt, 1/4 teaspoon pepper, and half the garlic in a large bowl. Using a pastry brush, coat the surface of the mushrooms, inside and out, with the oil mixture. Place the mushrooms on a baking sheet, domed side down. Bake for about 15 minutes, or until the centers of the mushrooms are tender. Drain the mushrooms on paper towels and set aside to cool. Keep the oven on.

To make the filling, in a large skillet, heat 2 tablespoons of the olive oil over high heat. When the oil is nearly smoking, add enough of the zucchini to make a single layer in the pan. Cook the zucchini without stirring until browned on one side, about 5 minutes. Stir the zucchini and cook for an additional 2 minutes, or until lightly browned on all sides. Remove to a medium bowl and repeat with the remaining zucchini.

Add the bell pepper, onion, and remaining tablespoon oil to the skillet and cook, without stirring, for 5 minutes, or until browned. Stir the mixture and cook for an additional 2 minutes. Add the bell pepper and onion to the zucchini.

Season the vegetable mixture with 1/4 teaspoon salt and pepper to taste. Let it cool in the refrigerator while preparing the rest of the filling.

Combine the cream cheese and butter in a medium bowl. Fold in the green onions, Parmesan cheese, sun-dried tomatoes, basil, parsley, remaining garlic, bread crumbs, and 1/4 teaspoon each salt and pepper. Mix the cheese mixture into the vegetable mixture, combining thoroughly but gently.

Place the mushrooms, domed side down, on a baking sheet. Divide the filling evenly among the mushroom caps, mounding it slightly. Push the filling to the edges to fill the entire cap. Top each with 3 slices tomato and sprinkle with the semisoft cheese, mounding it high.

Bake for about 20 minutes, or until the mushrooms are heated through and the cheese is melted and is beginning to brown.

MAKE AHEAD The stuffed mushrooms will keep for up to 3 days in the refrigerator. Reheat them, covered, in a 350°F. oven. The stuffing will keep for up to 5 days in the refrigerator.

Chuck Eggert

In the organic food world, few have contributed more than Chuck Eggert, president of Pacific Natural Foods in Tualatin, Oregon, a company that makes everything from soups and stocks to ready-to-eat meals. Chuck was the first in the country to bring natural, pure flavor products to the mass market. From the farmer to the soup pot, Chuck is involved in every aspect of his products.

Chuck started working in the food business when he was fifteen and eventually earned a degree in food science. After years in the business, Chuck started Pacific Natural Foods in 1987, producing soy and rice milk. Slowly the company moved into other areas, adding soups, stocks, and nut-based products. From the beginning, Chuck notes, the company has always made natural, organic foods. "The more we learned about what we were doing, the more it reinforced the fact that simpler is really better," Chuck says. "Many products have become overcomplicated. Reverting to tomatoes and milk for tomato soup is really simple. The more we've done it, the more we've realized we can make a better, higher-quality product from organic ingredients. Organic ingredients are so much more flavorful and easier to work with than their conventional counterparts."

Chuck's commitment to organic products has led him to move into the supply side as well, working with local farmers and even starting his own farm, Western Oregon Organic Farms. It is unusual for processors to get involved with the production of ingredients, but to Chuck, it's an important part of the business. Buying locally is also important to him. "We source 50 percent of our production from Oregon," he says. "I believe that having local agriculture, and especially sustainable, organic agriculture, helps farmers sell things and develop products." It also helps the company; as Chuck says, "The quicker we can get the milk, the higher the quality of the finished product. We're very concerned about where products come from. Could we find them cheaper? Probably, but we don't even look. We like to go back to the farmers and find the guy who grows the red peppers for us. We can tell you who grew them and where they came from." This dedication to the people behind the food extends to his work with the Oregon Food Bank. Chuck has dedicated production time to produce soup specifically for the Food Bank, and Pacific Natural soups and broths are sent to the Oregon Food Bank for distribution to food banks around the state.

Chuck is also a cofounder of New Seasons Market in Portland, Oregon, a specialty market that feels like an old-fashioned store, where everyone says hello and the staff answer questions about all the products. "I think there is a resurgence in people caring about where their food comes from. That's why there's a boom in the farmer's markets. People want to know their food didn't just come off the boat from somewhere," says Chuck.

BRAISED KALE GRATIN

SERVES 4 TO 6 AS A SIDE DISH

KALE SEEMS TO INTIMIDATE PEOPLE. Maybe it's the large dark green leaves and the tough thick stalks that spill over the grocery bins. Whatever the reason, it's a shame. Leafy kale is one of the most nutritious vegetables around and extremely versatile. This recipe takes a detour from the classic gratin: Brown rice replaces potatoes, and the earthiness of the kale creates a healthy, hearty side dish. You can use any variety of kale in this dish, but my favorite is the dinosaur variety for its full flavor.

$^3/_4$ cup short-grain brown rice

2 bunches dinosaur kale (about 10 leaves per bunch)

$2^1/_2$ tablespoons extra-virgin olive oil

1 small yellow onion, chopped

$^1/_2$ cup Chicken Stock (page 230) or store-bought low-sodium chicken broth

1 cup milk

$1^1/_2$ teaspoons kosher salt

$^1/_4$ teaspoon freshly ground black pepper

Pinch of nutmeg

1 large egg plus 1 large egg yolk

7 ounces semihard cheese (page 23), shredded ($1^3/_4$ cups)

$^1/_4$ cup fresh bread crumbs

Preheat the oven to 350°F. Butter an 8-inch baking dish.

Cook the rice according to the package instructions and set aside.

Wash the kale, strip the leaves from the stems, and cut the leaves into 1-inch strips. Bring a large pot of salted water to a boil. Blanch the kale for 2 minutes. Drain the kale and rinse to cool, squeezing out excess water. Set aside.

Heat the olive oil in a large saucepan over medium-high heat. Add the onion and cook for 4 minutes, or until it begins to brown. Add the chicken stock and boil for 3 minutes, or until the liquid is reduced to less than $^1/_4$ cup. Reduce the heat to medium-low and stir in the milk along with the salt, pepper, nutmeg, rice, and kale. Remove from the heat and stir in the egg, yolk, and $1^1/_2$ cups of the cheese, mixing thoroughly.

Spread the mixture in the baking dish and top with the reserved $^1/_4$ cup cheese and the bread crumbs. Bake for about 40 minutes, or until the gratin is golden brown on top and bubbling around the edges.

Serve hot or at room temperature.

MAKE AHEAD The gratin will keep, covered, for up to 5 days in the refrigerator and in the freezer for up to 3 months. Reheat, covered, in a 350°F. oven for 30 to 40 minutes.

STUFFED MUSTARD GREENS

THIS RECIPE WAS INSPIRED BY DOLMADES, the classic Greek appetizer. Mustard greens, a deliciously bitter leaf, stand in for grape leaves, and the earthiness of celery root and the bite of sheep's-milk cheese complete this healthy, hearty dish that your vegetarian—and nonvegetarian—friends will love. It's important to use fresh herbs instead of dried in this recipe because these ingredients aren't cooked and dried herbs wouldn't be fully reconstituted.

1½ cups short-grain brown rice

1¾ teaspoons kosher salt, plus more for sprinkling

1 small celery root, peeled and cut into ¼-inch pieces

¼ teaspoon freshly ground black pepper, plus more for sprinkling

1½ tablespoons extra-virgin olive oil

24 mustard green leaves (2 to 3 bunches mustard greens)

8 ounces semihard sheep's-milk cheese, diced (1½ cups)

8 green onions (white and green parts), chopped

¼ red bell pepper, diced

2 teaspoons chopped fresh rosemary

2 teaspoons chopped fresh thyme

2 tablespoons apple cider vinegar

Cook the rice according to package instructions with ½ teaspoon of the salt. Set aside.

Preheat the oven to 400°F.

In a medium bowl, combine the celery root, ¼ teaspoon of the salt, the pepper, and the olive oil. Pour the mixture onto a baking sheet. Roast for 12 to 15 minutes, or until the cubes are golden brown, stirring once.

While the celery root is roasting, blanch the mustard greens in a pot of salted boiling water for 2 minutes. Rinse the greens in cold water, drain well, and towel dry. Set aside.

In a large bowl, combine the rice, celery root, cheese, green onions, bell pepper, rosemary, thyme, vinegar, and 1 teaspoon salt.

To assemble the rolls, lay one leaf flat on a cutting board or other smooth surface. Using a sharp knife, slice the stem at the bottom of the leaf straight up the middle about 1 to 2 inches. (This helps the leaf fold more easily over the stuffing.) Sprinkle a pinch of salt and pepper over each leaf. In the middle of the leaf, place 2 tablespoons of the filling. Using your hands, shape the filling into a 1½ x ½-inch log lying alongside the stem of the leaf. Fold the short ends of the leaf over the filling. Fold one long side over the filling and then roll up the other side of the leaf, creating a small cylindrical package. Repeat with the remaining leaves and filling.

Serve at room temperature.

MAKE AHEAD The stuffed mustard greens taste best the day they are prepared, but you can assemble them 1 day ahead, cover, and refrigerate.

NOTE I prefer the stuffed mustard greens uncooked, but they can be heated in a steamer. To steam, create a single layer of rolls in the bottom of a steamer and steam for 7 minutes. Repeat until all of the rolls are steamed. Brush with olive oil and top with salt and pepper to taste before serving.

POTATOES AU GRATIN

THIS IS A RECIPE WE CREATED FOR BEECHER'S. Although it was popular, it didn't keep well in the store format so we stopped selling it, much to the disappointment of our loyal customers. We get asked for the recipe for this classic cheesy potato dish all the time, so here it is.

2 tablespoons unsalted butter

2$^{1}/_{2}$ tablespoons all-purpose flour

1$^{1}/_{2}$ cups milk

$^{1}/_{2}$ teaspoon kosher salt

2 large russet potatoes, peeled and thinly sliced (about 2 pounds)

8 ounces semihard cheese (page 23), grated (2 cups)

1 ounce semisoft cheese (page 23), grated ($^{1}/_{4}$ cup)

$^{1}/_{4}$ teaspoon chipotle chili powder

$^{1}/_{8}$ teaspoon garlic powder

$^{1}/_{4}$ cup fresh bread crumbs

Preheat the oven to 350°F. Butter an 8-inch baking dish.

Heat a medium saucepan over medium heat and melt the butter. Stir in the flour and cook for 1 minute. Add 1 cup of the milk and stir until smooth. Add the remaining $^{1}/_{2}$ cup milk and the salt. Add the potatoes to the milk mixture, stirring to coat. Cook the potatoes, stirring occasionally, for about 5 minutes. The potatoes should still be firm. (They will finish baking in the oven.) Remove from the heat.

Stir in 1$^{3}/_{4}$ cups of the semihard cheese along with the semisoft cheese, chipotle powder, and garlic powder. Pour the potato mixture into the baking dish, spreading it evenly. Top with the reserved $^{1}/_{4}$ cup semihard cheese and the bread crumbs.

Bake for about 45 minutes, or until the top is golden brown, the sauce is bubbly, and the potatoes in the center of the dish are tender when pierced with a fork.

Let the gratin cool for 5 minutes before serving.

MAKE AHEAD To make the gratin up to 1 day in advance, prepare it to the point of baking, cover, and refrigerate. Bake for about 1 hour. Reheat leftover gratin in a preheated 350°F. oven, covered with foil.

potatoes

Although almost every culture in the world embraces the potato, Americans in particular love this vegetable. Why else would we eat about 134 pounds of potatoes per person every year? Fried, baked, mashed, or roasted, this most versatile of vegetables welcomes whatever flavor you throw at it. Eastern Washington has acres and acres of potatoes growing in the rich volcanic soil. (And while Idaho claims potatoes for their own, farmers in Washington actually grow more potatoes than any other state—20 percent of the U.S. potato production.)

The humble potato comes in endless varieties. Everyone loves the russet (there are five varieties of the russet alone), and although it's known as the Idaho potato, it's actually grown throughout the Midwest. Russets are great for baking and frying, but the other varieties offer flavor and texture differences. There are whites (including White Rose and Cascade), reds (including Chieftain and Idarose), yellows (including creamy, buttery Yukon Golds), purples from Washington's Skagit Valley, and fingerlings (those waxy, flavorful potatoes named because their shape resembles large fingers). The term *new potatoes* means the potatoes are young and have less starch and wispy skins, making them the ideal choice for cooking whole.

Choose potatoes that are firm and free of bruises and sprouting. Keep them in a cool, dark place—the refrigerator is no friend to the potato—and don't wash them until you're ready to eat them. And there's really no need to peel potatoes—leave the skins on for a more rustic, and healthier, flavor.

RED, WHITE, AND GREEN VEGETABLE "LASAGNE"

SERVES 12 AS A SIDE DISH, 8 AS A MAIN COURSE

THIS COLORFUL CASSEROLE is reminiscent of lasagne, but it uses vegetables in place of pasta. It's a great main dish for vegetarians and does double duty as a vegetable side dish that is reminiscent of a starch dish. While the recipe requires several steps, each element can be made ahead and then assembled at the last minute.

2½ pounds red beets, peeled and thinly sliced, greens removed and reserved

1 tablespoon fresh thyme

1 tablespoon extra-virgin olive oil

Kosher salt and freshly ground black pepper

4 tablespoons (½ stick) unsalted butter

¼ cup all-purpose flour

2 cups milk

Dash of cayenne pepper

Dash of garlic powder

4 ounces semihard cheese (page 23), grated (1 cup)

4 ounces semisoft cheese (page 23), grated (1 cup)

½ cup fresh bread crumbs

4 ounces blue cheese (page 23), crumbled (1 cup)

½ head cauliflower, thinly sliced

Five-Onion Confit (recipe follows) or 1 cup store-bought onion-based chutney

Green Bean Pesto (page 246) or ¼ cup store-bought pesto

Preheat the oven to 425°F. Bring a large pot of salted water to a boil. Have ready a large bowl filled halfway with ice water.

In a large bowl, combine the beets, thyme, olive oil, ½ teaspoon salt, and ¼ teaspoon black pepper. Spread the beet mixture on a baking sheet. Roast for 25 minutes, stirring once, or until the beets are tender.

While the beets are roasting, remove the red stems from the reserved beet greens and discard. Blanch the leaves in the boiling water until they wilt and turn bright green, about 30 seconds. Transfer the greens to the bowl of ice water to cool. Drain the greens and squeeze them to remove any remaining moisture. Set aside.

In a large saucepan over medium heat, melt the butter and whisk in the flour. Slowly add the milk, whisking constantly. Add the cayenne, garlic powder, ½ teaspoon salt, and a dash of black pepper. Cook until the sauce thickens, about 10 minutes, stirring frequently. Remove from the heat. Add the semihard and semisoft cheeses and continue whisking until the cheese is completely melted. Set aside.

Remove the beets from the oven and set them aside. Reduce the oven heat to 375°F. Butter a 9 x 13-inch baking dish.

[RECIPE CONTINUES]

Sprinkle the bread crumbs over the bottom of the baking dish. Place half of the beets on top of the bread crumbs in one overlapping layer. Arrange half of the blue cheese in large chunks on top of the beets. Make a second layer with the remaining beets and blue cheese. Drizzle ¼ cup of the cheese sauce on top. Sprinkle with salt and black pepper. Place the beet greens on top of the cheese sauce. Sprinkle with salt and pepper. Layer the cauliflower, ¼ cup cheese sauce, and then the onion confit. Sprinkle with salt and pepper and top with the remaining cheese sauce, spreading it to the edges of the dish and covering any exposed confit.

Bake, uncovered, for 40 minutes. Let the lasagne sit for at least 20 minutes before slicing and serving.

Serve with a generous dollop of Green Bean Pesto.

Five-Onion Confit

MAKES ABOUT 1 CUP

This confit is truly versatile. It can be used as a thickener in a soup or sauce, a flavor and texture boost to potato salad, or a filling for pork or beef sandwiches.

2 tablespoons extra-virgin olive oil
1 medium red onion, thinly sliced
1 medium white onion, thinly sliced
1 medium yellow onion, thinly sliced
3 shallots, thinly sliced
1 large leek, chopped (see Note)

5 garlic cloves, chopped
1 tablespoon balsamic vinegar
³/₄ teaspoon kosher salt
¼ teaspoon freshly ground black pepper
1 teaspoon sugar

Heat the oil in a large saucepan over medium heat. Add the onions, shallots, leek, garlic, vinegar, salt, pepper, and sugar and stir. Cook the onion mixture, stirring occasionally, for 45 minutes. Reduce the heat to low and continue cooking for 15 minutes, or until the onions are soft and brown and reduced to about 1 cup.

MAKE AHEAD The confit will keep, covered, for up to 5 days in the refrigerator.

NOTE For tips on cleaning a leek, see page 24.

LEMON-CAPER CAULIFLOWER

SERVES 4 TO 6 AS A SIDE DISH

ANYONE WHO'S COOKED WITH ME KNOWS I LOVE CAPERS. (If I had my way, I'd write a caper cookbook.) Here's a dish I've made at home for years that we now sell at Pasta & Co. The rich flavor of cauliflower balances perfectly with the lemon and capers, while the red onion gives the dish a hint of color and a little crunch.

1 head cauliflower (approximately 2 pounds), cut into 1 1/2-inch florets

1/2 cup extra-virgin olive oil

1/2 small red onion, minced

1 1/2 tablespoons capers, drained and mashed

2 tablespoons pureed preserved lemon (see Note)

1 1/2 tablespoons freshly squeezed lemon juice

2 1/4 teaspoons kosher salt

1 1/4 teaspoons freshly ground black pepper

1/4 cup chopped fresh flat-leaf parsley

Bring a large stockpot of salted water to a boil. Add the cauliflower and cook for 2 minutes, or until tender. (A fork should easily pierce the cauliflower but not break it apart.) Drain the cauliflower and rinse it under cold water.

Combine the olive oil, onion, capers, preserved lemon, lemon juice, salt, and pepper in a large bowl. Add the cauliflower and mix well. Marinate for at least 1 hour at room temperature, tossing once or twice.

Garnish with the parsley and serve at room temperature.

MAKE AHEAD The cauliflower will keep, covered, for 2 days in the refrigerator; toss it again before serving.

NOTE Preserved lemons are a staple of Moroccan cuisine. The lemons are packed in jars with salt for about a month until most of the moisture has been drawn out and the lemons have softened. The sour and salty flavors combine with a hint of sweetness that works well in both savory and sweet dishes. Just remember to rinse the lemons before use. You can find preserved lemons in most specialty food stores. If you can't find them, substitute 2 tablespoons lemon juice, 1/2 teaspoon sugar, and kosher salt to taste.

Frank Isernio

Frank Isernio started making fresh sausage as a hobby in his home kitchen for his southern Italian family and friends who couldn't find a supply of fresh sausage in the Seattle area. He soon moved his operation to the basement of a friend's house, and, after working his shift at the shipyard, he would pack the sausage in the trunk of his car and sell it to local restaurants. Today, Isernio Sausage Company makes fifteen varieties of all-natural, nitrate-free sausage that are sold to restaurants and grocery stores in the Pacific Northwest.

"We were always natural, from day one," says Frank. "We took it for granted that you had to be. We were not touting it, but then we realized people were aware of additives and healthy eating, so we changed our packaging to include the words 'all-natural.'" His first grocery store customers labeled his product "gourmet sausage" to differentiate it from commodity sausage. "We told them, 'This is whole muscle meat, this is lean, there are no chemicals, and we use natural casings,'" says Frank.

What sets Frank apart is that he makes fresh sausages without preservatives—and his sausages, which have a shelf life of only a few days, are a local favorite. As Frank points out, there's no need to add preservatives to fresh sausage because it's meant to be eaten within a few days.

Three kinds of sausage are available to consumers: fresh sausage, meaning fresh meat with spices that is meant to be eaten in a few days; precooked sausage; and cured sausage, such as salami. Fresh sausage has long been common in European markets, where the butchers traditionally serve a small territory and don't have to ship their product. "Preservatives shouldn't be a part of fresh sausage," says Frank.

Because fresh sausage is so perishable, Isernio's products are available only in the Pacific Northwest and Hawaii. Try it on your next trip out west. But don't despair; Frank is busy creating frozen products that are available nationwide—preservative-free and all natural, as always.

SAUSAGE-OYSTER STUFFING

SERVES 4 TO 6 AS A SIDE DISH

SWEET, SALTY OYSTERS AND SPICY SAUSAGE are the stars of this classic American stuffing. This is great for Thanksgiving and perfect with most meat or poultry dishes.

12 ounces artisanal sourdough bread
   (about 1 medium loaf)

12 ounces mild Italian chicken or pork
   sausage, casings removed

2 tablespoons (¼ stick) unsalted butter

½ large yellow onion, chopped

1½ large celery ribs, chopped

2 garlic cloves, minced

2¼ teaspoons fresh thyme or
   ¾ teaspoon dried

1 tablespoon chopped fresh sage or
   1 teaspoon dried

2 teaspoons chopped fresh marjoram or
   ½ teaspoon dried

⅛ teaspoon cayenne pepper

1 10-ounce jar oysters or 5 fresh oysters,
   liquor reserved

½ teaspoon kosher salt

¼ teaspoon freshly ground black pepper

2 ounces semihard cheese (page 23),
   shredded (½ cup)

1 to 2 cups Turkey Stock (page 231),
   Chicken Stock (page 230), or store-
   bought low-sodium chicken broth

Preheat the oven to 325°F.

Cut the bread into ½-inch cubes and spread them on two baking sheets. Bake for about 30 minutes, stirring occasionally, or until the cubes are dry and light brown. Set aside to cool.

Sauté the sausage in a medium skillet over medium heat, breaking up the meat into 1-inch pieces, for 10 minutes, or until lightly browned and cooked through. Set aside.

In the same skillet, reduce the heat to medium-low and melt the butter. Add the onion, celery, garlic, thyme, sage, marjoram, and cayenne and cook until the onion mixture begins to soften but not brown, about 4 minutes. Remove from the heat.

Increase the oven temperature to 375°F. and butter an 8-inch baking dish.

Put the bread in a large bowl. Drain the oysters over the bread. On a cutting board, chop the oysters into 1-inch pieces. Add the oysters to the bread along with the onion mixture, sausage, salt, pepper, and half of the cheese. Drizzle half of the stock over the mixture and toss gently. Let sit for 5 minutes to absorb the stock. Add enough additional stock to make the bread moist but not soggy. (You might not use all of the stock.)

Pour the mixture into the baking dish and pat it down. Sprinkle with the remaining cheese and cover with foil. Bake for 30 minutes, uncover, and bake for another 10 to 15 minutes, or until the cheese is melted and the top is beginning to brown. Serve warm.

MAKE AHEAD The cooked stuffing will keep for up to 3 days ahead in the refrigerator or in the freezer for up to 1 month. Reheat it in a covered baking dish at 375°F. for 30 minutes.

WILD MUSHROOM STUFFING

SERVES 4 TO 6 AS A SIDE DISH

THE PACIFIC NORTHWEST HAS A CORNUCOPIA OF MUSHROOMS: morels and porcini in the spring, chanterelles and black trumpets in the fall and winter, and fresh shiitakes all year round. Earthy mushrooms bring a new dimension to stuffing. Serve the mushroom stuffing with Kale-Stuffed Chicken Breasts (page 118) or on its own as a vegetarian main course.

12 ounces artisanal sourdough bread (about 1 medium loaf)

1 ounce dried shiitake mushrooms

3½ tablespoons unsalted butter

7 ounces fresh mushrooms, such as crimini and chanterelles, wiped clean

3 tablespoons pale dry sherry

½ large yellow onion, diced

1½ large celery ribs, diced

2 garlic cloves, minced

2 teaspoons fresh thyme or 1¼ teaspoons dried

1½ teaspoons chopped fresh sage or ¾ teaspoon dried

2 teaspoons fresh marjoram, chopped, or 1 teaspoon dried

1 teaspoon kosher salt

½ teaspoon freshly ground black pepper

2 ounces semihard grating cheese (page 23), shredded (½ cup)

½ cup Turkey Stock (page 231), Chicken Stock (page 230), or store-bought low-sodium chicken or vegetable broth

Preheat the oven to 325°F.

Cut the bread into ½-inch cubes and arrange them on two baking sheets. Bake for about 30 minutes, stirring occasionally, until the cubes are dry and light brown. Set aside.

Bring 2 cups water to a boil in a small saucepan. Add the dried shiitakes and stir to submerge them. Remove the pan from the heat, cover, and let the mushrooms steep for 30 minutes. Strain the broth into a measuring cup. You will need 1½ cups of the broth for the stuffing; reserve aside. Cut off and discard the stems from the shiitakes. Thinly slice the caps and reserve.

While the mushrooms are steeping, heat a medium skillet over medium-high heat and melt 1½ tablespoons of the butter. Add the fresh mushrooms and let them cook without stirring for 2 to 3 minutes, or until some of the mushrooms are beginning to brown. Stir the mushrooms and cook until the liquid has evaporated, 3 to 5 minutes. Add the sherry and simmer for 2 minutes. Remove the mixture to a bowl and set aside.

Return the skillet to the stove over medium-low heat and melt the remaining 2 tablespoons butter in it. Add the onion, celery, garlic, thyme, sage, and marjoram. Cook until the onion mixture begins to soften but not brown, about 4 minutes. Remove from the heat.

Increase the oven heat to 375°F. and butter an 8-inch baking dish.

To assemble, use your hands to toss the bread with the cooked mushrooms, shiitakes, onion mixture, salt, pepper, and half of the cheese in a large bowl. In a separate bowl, combine the 1½ cups mushroom broth with the stock. Drizzle half the liquid over the bread mixture while gently tossing. Let sit for 3 to 5 minutes for the bread to absorb the liquid. Continue to gently toss the bread mixture, adding enough liquid to make the bread moist but not soggy. (You might not use all of the liquid.)

Pour the bread mixture into the baking dish and pat it down. Sprinkle the stuffing with the remaining cheese and cover it with a piece of lightly buttered aluminum foil. Bake for 30 minutes and then uncover and bake for another 10 to 15 minutes, or until the cheese is melted and the top layer is just beginning to brown. Serve warm.

MAKE AHEAD The stuffing will keep, covered, for up to 3 days in the refrigerator.

APPLE-PECAN STUFFING
with Dried Cherries

SERVES 4 TO 6 AS A SIDE DISH

THIS SWEET AND SAVORY STUFFING offers a textural element in every bite. It is a perfect side for poultry dishes.

12 ounces artisanal sourdough bread
    (about 1 medium loaf)
1 large or 2 medium sweet apples, such
    as Fuji
6 tablespoons ($^3/_4$ stick) unsalted butter
$^1/_2$ large yellow onion, chopped
2 large celery ribs, chopped
1 tablespoon fresh thyme or 1 teaspoon
    dried
1 tablespoon chopped fresh sage or
    1 teaspoon dried
1 tablespoon chopped fresh marjoram
    or 1 teaspoon dried

1 cup dried sour or sweet cherries
$^1/_2$ cup pecan pieces, lightly toasted
    (page 195)
$^1/_2$ teaspoon kosher salt
$^1/_4$ teaspoon freshly ground black pepper
About 1 cup apple juice
1 cup Turkey Stock (page 231), Chicken
    Stock (page 230), or store-bought low-
    sodium chicken or vegetable broth
1 ounce Parmesan or other hard cheese
    (page 23), shredded ($^1/_4$ cup)

Preheat the oven to 325°F.

Cut the bread into $^1/_2$-inch cubes and spread them on two baking sheets. Bake for about 30 minutes, stirring occasionally, or until the cubes are dry and light brown. Set aside to cool.

While the bread is baking, peel, quarter, and core the apples and cut them into $^1/_2$-inch pieces.

In a medium skillet over medium-high heat, melt 3 tablespoons of the butter and sauté the apples until their edges begin to brown, about 4 minutes. Remove the apples to a bowl and set aside to cool.

Reduce the heat to medium-low and melt the remaining 3 tablespoons butter in the skillet. Add the onion, celery, thyme, sage, and marjoram and cook until the onion mixture begins to soften but not brown, about 4 minutes. Remove from the heat.

Increase the oven temperature to 375°F. and butter an 8-inch baking dish.

In a large bowl, use your hands to toss the bread with the onion mixture, apples, cherries, pecans, salt, and pepper. Drizzle half of the apple juice and stock over the bread mixture while gently tossing. Let sit for 3 to 5 minutes to allow the mixture to absorb the liquid. Continue to gently toss the bread mixture, adding enough liquid to make the bread moist but not soggy. (You might not use all of the liquid.)

Pour the bread mixture into the baking dish and pat it down, pressing any cherries that are on top down into the stuffing. (If you leave the cherries exposed, they will burn.) Sprinkle the stuffing with the cheese and cover with a piece of lightly buttered aluminum foil.

Bake for 30 minutes and then uncover and bake for another 10 to 15 minutes, or until the cheese is melted and the top is just beginning to brown. Serve warm.

MAKE AHEAD The stuffing will keep, covered, for up to 3 days in the refrigerator. Reheat it in a covered baking dish at 375°F. for approximately 30 minutes. Uncover for the last 5 minutes for a crispier top.

SWEETS

CHOCOLATE TRUFFLE COOKIES

GINGER CRINKLES

GIANT SNICKERDOODLES

APRICOT BARS

STRAWBERRY-RHUBARB BARS

STRAWBERRY SHORTCAKE WITH FROMAGE BLANC
WHIPPED CREAM

TWO-APPLE CRISPS WITH CARAMEL SAUCE

SUMMER BERRY PARFAIT

PARSNIP SPICE CAKE

HAZELNUT TORTE

PEAR-GINGER PIE

MOCHA–BUTTER CRUNCH PIE

HONEY BLANK SLATE CHEESECAKE

CHOCOLATE TRUFFLE COOKIES

MAKES 45 COOKIES

IF YOU KNOW A CHOCOHOLIC, THEN START BAKING. These intense chocolate cookies are made with three types of chocolate—unsweetened, semisweet, and cocoa powder—for maximum flavor, but have a light-as-air texture. They are incredibly satisfying without being dense or heavy.

4 ounces unsweetened chocolate	$1/4$ teaspoon baking powder
6 tablespoons ($3/4$ stick) unsalted butter	$1/4$ teaspoon table salt
2 cups semisweet chocolate chips	3 large eggs
$1/2$ cup plus 1 tablespoon all-purpose flour	1 cup sugar
$1/2$ teaspoon cocoa powder	$1^1/2$ teaspoons vanilla extract

Chop the unsweetened chocolate into $1/2$-inch pieces and place them in a medium metal bowl with the butter and 1 cup of the chocolate chips. Fill a medium saucepan with 1 inch hot water and heat over medium-low heat. Place the metal bowl on top of the saucepan and melt the chocolate, stirring occasionally. (Alternatively, you can melt the chocolate mixture in a double boiler or in a microwave-safe bowl in the microwave in 15-second spurts.) Once the chocolate is melted, remove it from the heat.

In a medium bowl, sift together the flour, cocoa powder, baking powder, and salt.

Using a handheld mixer or stand mixer fitted with the flat beater attachment, beat the eggs and sugar on medium speed until thick and light in color. Mix in the vanilla and the melted chocolate mixture until fully combined. Scrape the bowl once or twice while mixing. Add the dry ingredients to the mixing bowl. Mix on low speed to incorporate the flour, scraping the bowl once or twice. Fold in the remaining 1 cup chocolate chips. Let the cookie dough rest for approximately 30 minutes.

Meanwhile, preheat the oven to 350°F. and grease a baking sheet.

Roll the cookie dough into 1-inch balls and drop them 2 inches apart onto the baking sheet. With the palm of your hand, lightly flatten the dough balls; this will help them bake evenly.

Bake for 8 to 10 minutes, or until the cookies are shiny and darker in the center. Watch them carefully so you can pull them as soon as they turn shiny; this guarantees a gooey center. Cool the cookies on the baking sheet for 5 minutes before carefully transferring them to a cooling rack with a spatula.

MAKE AHEAD The cookies will keep in an airtight container at room temperature for up to 5 days.

GINGER CRINKLES

MAKES 36 COOKIES

IF YOU THINK YOU DON'T LIKE GINGER, these cookies are sure to change your mind. With cloves, cinnamon, and ginger, these soft, chewy cookies have a bite all their own. Ground ginger has a more intense flavor than fresh and is ideal for baking. The only way to improve on these cookies is to sandwich vanilla ice cream between pairs of them. (See photograph on page 174.)

2¼ cups all-purpose flour
¼ teaspoon table salt
2 teaspoons baking soda
2 teaspoons ground cinnamon
1½ teaspoons ground ginger
½ teaspoon ground cloves
1 large egg

½ cup neutral-flavored cooking oil, such as canola or soybean
3 tablespoons unsalted butter, melted
¼ cup plus 1½ tablespoons blackstrap molasses (see Note)
1 cup packed light brown sugar
½ cup granulated sugar

Preheat the oven to 375°F.

In a large bowl, sift together the flour, salt, baking soda, cinnamon, ginger, and cloves.

Using a handheld mixer or stand mixer fitted with the flat beater attachment, mix together the egg, oil, butter, molasses, and brown sugar at medium speed, scraping the bowl once or twice while mixing. Add the dry ingredients to the mixing bowl. Mix at low speed to incorporate the flour. Scrape the bowl once or twice while mixing. Stop mixing as soon as the dough is uniform.

Place the granulated sugar in a shallow medium bowl. Form the dough into 1½-inch balls and roll 4 to 6 balls at a time in the sugar until each ball is completely covered in sugar. Place the balls 2 inches apart on an ungreased baking sheet.

Bake the cookies for 8 to 10 minutes for a chewy cookie. For a crisper cookie, bake for 12 minutes. Cool the cookies on the baking sheet for 5 minutes before carefully transferring them to a cooling rack to cool completely.

MAKE AHEAD The cookies will keep in an airtight container at room temperature for up to 5 days.

NOTE Blackstrap molasses makes the cookies darker and gives them a richer flavor than regular molasses. It is also full of vitamins and minerals, making it more nutritious than many other sweeteners. You can find blackstrap molasses at most grocery stores, but you can substitute light or dark molasses if you prefer.

GIANT SNICKERDOODLES

MAKES 3 10-INCH COOKIES OR 36 SMALL COOKIES (SEE NOTE)

SNICKERDOODLE IS ANOTHER NAME FOR a vanilla butter cookie covered in cinnamon sugar. Light and soft in texture, they're simple to make. Cut them into shapes, such as triangles, before baking and dip the pieces in melted chocolate once they're cool for a fun dessert. They also make the perfect cookie for ice cream sandwiches. (See photograph on page 174.)

3 cups all-purpose flour	2 cups plus 3 tablespoons sugar
$1/2$ teaspoon baking soda	2 large eggs
1 teaspoon cream of tartar	2 tablespoons milk
1 teaspoon table salt	1 teaspoon vanilla extract
1 cup (2 sticks) unsalted butter, softened	1 tablespoon ground cinnamon

Preheat the oven to 375°F. Grease 1 or 2 baking sheets and set aside.

In a medium bowl, combine the flour, baking soda, cream of tartar, and salt. Set aside.

Using a handheld mixer or stand mixer fitted with the flat beater attachment, beat the butter and 2 cups of the sugar on medium speed until fluffy, scraping the bowl once or twice while mixing. In a medium bowl, combine the eggs, milk, and vanilla. Slowly pour the liquid into the butter mixture while the mixer is running. Add the dry ingredients to the mixing bowl. Mix on low speed to incorporate the flour, scraping the bowl once or twice while mixing and stopping as soon as the dough is uniform.

In a large, shallow bowl, combine the remaining 3 tablespoons sugar and the cinnamon. Separate the dough into 3 portions. Roll each portion into one large ball and roll the ball in the cinnamon mixture until it is completely covered.

Place 1 ball of dough in the center of a baking sheet and, using the flat of your hand moistened with water, press down to flatten it into a $1/4$-inch-thick by 10-inch-wide disk. Because you can bake only one cookie per baking sheet, you can speed the process by baking 2 cookies on 2 baking sheets at the same time. Bake each cookie for 20 to 24 minutes, until the cookie is soft and springy in the middle and crispy around the edges.

Cool each cookie on the baking sheet for 5 minutes before carefully transferring it to a cooling rack with a spatula. Let cool completely.

NOTE To make about 36 $2^1/2$-inch thin, crisp cookies, roll the dough into 1-inch balls, roll them in the cinnamon sugar, and drop them 2 inches apart onto a greased baking sheet. Flatten them into $1/4$-inch-thick disks and bake for 9 to 12 minutes. For a thicker cookie, add an extra $1/2$ cup flour.

MAKE AHEAD The cookies will keep in an airtight container at room temperature for up to 5 days.

APRICOT BARS

THE KEY TO THESE SWEET AND CHUNKY apricot bars is using the highest-quality apricot preserves possible. Look for the word *preserves* on the label rather than *jam* or *jelly*; preserves have more fruit chunks. (Artificial colors are sometimes added to apricot jams, jelly, and preserves, so check the list of ingredients on the label.) These are a great dessert for a picnic or a bake sale because they're easy to transport and stay fresh for days.

1 cup (2 sticks) unsalted butter, softened	$^1/_2$ teaspoon table salt
1 cup sugar	1 cup chopped walnuts
2 large egg yolks	$1^1/_4$ cups apricot preserves
2 cups all-purpose flour	

Preheat the oven to 350°F.

Using a hand held mixer or stand mixer with the flat beater attachment, beat the butter and sugar together until light and fluffy. Blend in the egg yolks 1 at a time. Scrape down the sides of the bowl and add the flour and salt, mixing well. Scrape the bowl again, add the walnuts, and stir until the mixture is thoroughly blended.

Spread two-thirds of the dough into a 9 x 13-inch baking pan, using lightly floured hands to pat and distribute the mixture evenly. The dough should be about $^3/_8$ inch thick. Wrap the remaining dough in plastic wrap and place it in the freezer.

Bake the crust for approximately 35 minutes, or until it is light golden brown in the middle, golden on the edges, and lightly springy in the center. Spread the apricot preserves evenly over the warm crust, just to the edges but not touching the sides of the pan. Using the large holes of a box grater, shred the chilled remaining dough evenly over the apricot preserves. Return to the oven and bake for another 25 to 30 minutes, or until the topping is light golden brown.

Let the bars cool for 1 hour and then cut them into 24 squares.

MAKE AHEAD The bars can be stored, covered, at room temperature for up to 5 days.

STRAWBERRY-RHUBARB BARS

MAKES 16 BARS

MORE RHUBARB IS GROWN IN THE PACIFIC NORTHWEST than in any other region of the country, meaning you'll often see rhubarb on dessert menus in local restaurants from April through September. Although rhubarb is technically a vegetable, its tart flavor lends itself to being treated like a fruit. Adding sugar and cooking the thick stalks softens the flavor. Strawberries and rhubarb are a classic combination, and they're even better accented with a little orange zest. These bars are a perfect portable dessert for lunchboxes and picnic baskets.

1½ cups plus 3 to 4 tablespoons all-purpose flour

¼ cup plus 2 tablespoons powdered sugar

½ teaspoon table salt

12 tablespoons (1½ sticks) cold unsalted butter, cut into 8 pieces

¾ cup plus ⅓ cup granulated sugar

⅛ teaspoon ground cloves

1 teaspoon grated orange zest

½ teaspoon vanilla extract

1½ pounds rhubarb, cut into ½-inch pieces (about 6 cups)

1½ cups strawberries, hulled and sliced, or frozen strawberries, thawed and sliced

Preheat the oven to 350°F.

In a large bowl, combine 1½ cups of the flour and the powdered sugar and salt. Cut the butter into the flour mixture using a pastry blender or fork. The mixture should resemble coarse crumbs and clump together when squeezed lightly in your hand. (This can also be done in a food processor.) Scoop 2 cups of the mixture into an 8-inch baking dish and press evenly into the pan with your fingers. Bake on the middle rack of the oven for 25 minutes, or until golden brown on the edges and light golden in the middle.

While the crust is baking, add ⅓ cup of the granulated sugar to the remaining butter-flour mixture and toss to combine. Set aside.

In a large bowl, combine ¾ cup granulated sugar and the ground cloves. Stir in 3 to 4 tablespoons flour (adding more flour will make the filling firmer when cool), the orange zest, and vanilla. Add the rhubarb and strawberries, mixing well to coat the fruit. Pour the mixture onto the hot crust, spreading the filling to the edges of the dish. Sprinkle the reserved sugar mixture over the fruit. Bake for 50 minutes or until bubbling around the edges and light brown on top.

Let the bars cool to room temperature before cutting and serving.

MAKE AHEAD The bars can be stored, covered, at room temperature for up to 5 days.

NOTE The bars are delicious served warm, but the filling won't be completely set and may be a little runny.

STRAWBERRY SHORTCAKE
with Fromage Blanc Whipped Cream

SERVES 6

THIS IS A FAMILY FAVORITE. We use a scone-like shortbread with a kick of orange zest as the base and Beecher's Blank Slate cheese, which contrasts nicely with the sweetness of the strawberries and the rich, buttery flavor of the shortcake. Any tart fresh cheese, such as fromage blanc, will work, or leave out the cheese and use 1½ cups heavy cream.

2 cups all-purpose flour

5 tablespoons plus ½ teaspoon sugar

1 tablespoon baking powder

½ teaspoon kosher salt

4 tablespoons (½ stick) cold unsalted
    butter, cut into ¼-inch pieces

2 cups heavy cream

1¾ teaspoons vanilla extract

¾ teaspoon grated orange zest

4 cups (about 2 pints) fresh strawberries,
    hulled and thinly sliced

6 ounces fromage blanc (¾ cup)

For the shortcake, sift the flour, 2 tablespoons plus 1 teaspoon of the sugar, the baking powder, and the salt into the bowl of a food processor. (Alternatively, you can make the dough using a pastry cutter.) Pulse to combine. Add the butter to the flour mixture and pulse just until the butter pieces become the size of peas. Combine 1 cup less 2 teaspoons of the cream, 1 teaspoon of the vanilla, and orange zest in a small bowl and add to the dough. Pulse until the dough is just combined, 6 to 8 pulses. Remove the dough from the food processor and knead gently once or twice to form a ball.

On a parchment-lined baking sheet, pat the dough into a 6 x 9-inch rectangle, approximately ¾ inch thick. Cover with plastic wrap and chill for 30 minutes.

Preheat the oven to 425°F.

Remove the dough from the refrigerator and straighten the edges by pushing on them with the flat side of a large knife, such as a chef's knife. Cut the rectangle into 6 even squares (2 squares by 3 squares) and arrange the squares 2 inches apart on the baking sheet. Using a pastry brush, brush them with 2 teaspoons cream and sprinkle the tops with 1 teaspoon sugar. Bake for 20 minutes or until the shortcakes are golden brown. Remove them from the baking sheet and let cool at least 5 minutes on a wire rack.

While the shortcakes bake, place the strawberries in a bowl and toss them with 1 tablespoon sugar. Cover and set aside.

For the topping, whip the remaining cup of cream in a bowl until soft peaks form. Add 1½ tablespoons sugar and ¾ teaspoon vanilla and stir gently. In another bowl, vigorously stir the cheese to soften it. Fold the whipped cream into the cheese. Refrigerate the topping until ready to use, up to 2 hours before serving.

When the shortcakes have cooled slightly, split them in half. Spoon about ½ cup strawberries over the bottom halves. Place a generous dollop of topping over the fruit and top with the other half of the shortcake. Finish with a small spoonful of topping and a couple of strawberry slices.

TWO-APPLE CRISPS
with Caramel Sauce

SERVES 8

THERE ARE MANY WAYS TO SHOW OFF APPLES in desserts, but warm apple crisps are always a favorite. Nine varieties of apple are grown in Washington State, including Gala, Braeburn, Cripps Pink, and Granny Smith. Use a mixture of your favorite apples, including one sweet variety, such as Fuji or Jonagold, and a more tart variety, such as Granny Smith or Cripps Pink. If you'd prefer to make one large crisp, use a 9 x 13-inch baking dish.

1 cup packed light brown sugar
1/3 cup all-purpose flour
3/4 cup old-fashioned rolled oats
1 1/2 teaspoons ground cinnamon
1/2 teaspoon table salt, plus a pinch for the apples
8 tablespoons (1 stick) cold unsalted butter, cut into pieces
1 1/2 pounds Golden Delicious apples (about 3 large apples), peeled, cored, and thinly sliced

1 1/2 pounds Granny Smith apples (about 3 large apples), peeled, cored, and thinly sliced
1/4 cup granulated sugar
1 teaspoon freshly squeezed lemon juice
Pinch of nutmeg
Caramel Sauce (opposite)

Preheat the oven to 350°F.

To make the topping, combine the brown sugar, flour, oats, cinnamon, and 1/2 teaspoon salt in a medium bowl. Using a fork, cut in the butter until the mixture resembles coarse crumbs. Set aside until ready to use.

In a large bowl, toss the apples with the granulated sugar, lemon juice, nutmeg, and a pinch of salt. Divide the apples among 8 ramekins, mounding them. Cover the apples with the oat topping, pressing the mixture lightly onto the apples. Make sure the apples are completely covered by the topping.

Bake for 45 minutes, or until the topping is golden brown and the apples are tender when pierced with a fork. Let the crisps cool for 5 minutes before serving. Drizzle each one with caramel sauce.

Caramel Sauce

MAKES ABOUT 1¼ CUPS

Besides serving this with the apple crisps, we use it as a sauce for cheesecake (see page 201). This basic caramel sauce also tastes great over ice cream.

½ cup plus 2 tablespoons granulated or
  turbinado sugar
1¼ cups heavy cream

¼ teaspoon table salt
1 teaspoon vanilla extract

Pour 6 tablespoons water into a heavy-bottomed 2-quart saucepan. Add the sugar and heat over medium-high, occasionally swirling the water gently, until the sugar melts, about 3 minutes.

While the sugar is cooking, bring the cream and salt to a simmer in a separate small, covered saucepan over medium-low heat, stirring occasionally. As soon as the mixture starts to simmer, remove it from the heat.

Once the sugar is completely melted, raise the heat to high and boil it for 6 to 10 minutes, or until the mixture turns the color of straw. Reduce the heat to medium and continue to cook for 2 minutes, or until the syrup is a deep amber color. (Pay close attention during these last 2 minutes of cooking so the syrup does not burn.)

Remove the pan from the heat and carefully pour about one-third of the hot cream into the caramel. The mixture will bubble vigorously. Let the bubbling subside and add the remaining hot cream and the vanilla, whisking until smooth. Serve warm.

MAKE AHEAD The sauce will keep in an airtight container for 2 weeks in the refrigerator. Reheat gently in a small saucepan over low heat until warm and melted.

SUMMER BERRY PARFAIT

THERE IS NO BETTER BOUNTY OF NORTHWEST SUMMERS than local berries. Strawberries arrive first, followed in rapid succession by raspberries, blueberries, blackberries, and cherries. (Cherries are technically a stone fruit, but to locals they are the grand marshal in our parade of summer berries.) Try any of these fruits in this easy parfait. Sliced peaches and nectarines are a welcome addition; whatever fruit is at its peak in the market will be your best choice. The addition of simple syrup enhances the natural sweetness of the fruit and adds a beautiful gloss. You can make the syrup ahead and refrigerate it in a sealed container for a week. This is a simple, elegant dessert—perfect for a relaxed summer evening.

$1/4$ cup sugar	2 cups fresh strawberries, hulled and
1 teaspoon vanilla extract	quartered
1 cup sour cream	1 cup fresh raspberries
$1/2$ cup heavy cream	1 cup fresh blueberries
2 tablespoons honey	$1/2$ cup crunchy granola

Make the simple syrup by combining the sugar, $1/4$ cup water, and $1/2$ teaspoon of the vanilla in a small saucepan over medium heat. Bring to a boil and stir until all the sugar is dissolved, about 5 minutes. Remove from the heat and cool to room temperature.

Combine the sour cream, heavy cream, honey, and remaining $1/2$ teaspoon vanilla in a small bowl with a whisk or fork. Set aside.

Place the strawberries, raspberries, and blueberries in 3 separate small bowls. Set aside 4 berries for garnish. Add approximately half of the simple syrup to the strawberries and mix gently with a flexible spatula so as not to bruise the fruit. Divide the remaining syrup between the raspberries and blueberries, mixing gently.

To assemble each parfait, place 1 tablespoon of the granola in the bottom of each of 4 glasses, breaking up any big chunks with your fingers. Top with the strawberries and a layer of cream. (Use about $1/2$ cup total of the cream, smoothing it to the edge of the glasses with a spoon.) Add a layer of blueberries and another layer of cream, followed by a layer of raspberries. Finish with a final dollop of cream.

Top each parfait with some of the remaining granola and the remaining reserved berries. Refrigerate until ready to serve, up to 2 hours.

PARSNIP SPICE CAKE

MAKES 1 9-INCH ROUND CAKE OR ABOUT 2 DOZEN CUPCAKES

PARSNIPS HAVE A DEEPER, MORE SOULFUL FLAVOR than carrots, and this hearty root vegetable takes center stage in our version of a carrot cake. Sweet and spiced with ginger and cloves, this moist cake makes a great birthday cake or anytime cake.

2 large eggs

1/2 cup neutral-flavored cooking oil, such as canola or soybean

1 cup sugar

1 teaspoon baking soda

1/2 teaspoon table salt

1 teaspoon ground ginger

Pinch of ground cloves

2 cups very coarsely grated parsnip (2 to 3 medium parsnips)

1/3 cup roughly chopped dried sour or sweet cherries or dried cranberries, plus extra for garnish

1/2 cup walnut pieces (optional)

1 cup all-purpose flour

Cream Cheese Frosting (recipe follows)

Preheat the oven to 350°F. Grease a 9-inch round cake pan or two 12-cup muffin tins (or line the muffin tins with cupcake papers).

In a medium bowl, whisk together the eggs, oil, sugar, baking soda, salt, ginger, and cloves. Add the parsnips, cherries or cranberries, and walnuts and whisk thoroughly. Stir in the flour and mix until fully combined. Pour the batter into the cake pan or fill the muffin tins three-quarters full. Bake until a toothpick inserted into the center comes out clean, 20 minutes for cupcakes or 40 minutes for a cake. Let cool for 5 minutes in the pan before inverting onto a cooling rack to cool completely.

Frost with the cream cheese frosting and garnish with additional cherries.

MAKE AHEAD The cake or cupcakes can be stored, covered, for up 3 days at room temperature or 5 days in the refrigerator.

Cream Cheese Frosting

MAKES ABOUT 1 1/2 CUPS

6 tablespoons (3/4 stick) unsalted butter, softened

8 ounces cream cheese, softened

3/4 teaspoon vanilla extract

2 teaspoons freshly squeezed lemon juice

About 3/4 cup powdered sugar, sifted

Beat the butter in a small bowl and add the cream cheese. Mix until thoroughly blended, scraping the sides of the bowl while stirring. Stir in the vanilla and lemon juice. Add the powdered sugar, 1/4 cup at a time. Taste after each addition for sweetness. Add more powdered sugar until the desired level of sweetness is reached.

MAKE AHEAD The frosting can be stored in an airtight container for up to 1 week in the refrigerator. Bring to room temperature before using.

HAZELNUT TORTE

MAKES 1 9-INCH ROUND TORTE

OUR EXECUTIVE CHEF AND PASTRY GURU (and hazelnut lover) Lura Smith has made this rich, dense torte for fifteen years to celebrate the hazelnuts of the region. The torte is made with agave syrup, a natural substitute for corn syrup. Agave syrup is available at specialty grocery stores.

3 large eggs

3 large egg yolks

3/4 cup sugar

3/4 cup agave syrup or corn syrup

4 tablespoons (1/2 stick) unsalted butter, melted

1/2 teaspoon table salt

13/4 cups hazelnuts, toasted, skins removed (page 195)

3 ounces chopped semisweet chocolate (1/2 cup)

Short Pie Crust Dough (recipe follows)

Position a rack in the lower third of the oven and preheat the oven to 400°F.

Whisk together the eggs, egg yolks, sugar, agave syrup, butter, and salt.

Sprinkle the hazelnuts and chocolate over the prepared pie crust. Pour the egg mixture over the hazelnuts and chocolate, stirring gently to combine. Bake for 10 minutes. Reduce the oven temperature to 350°F. and continue to bake for 45 minutes, or until the filling is puffed up on the edges, feels solid in the center when touched, and the crust is golden brown.

Let the torte cool completely without cutting before serving. (Cooling the pie allows the center filling to set.)

MAKE AHEAD The torte can be made 1 day ahead, and the crust can be refrigerated for up to 2 days.

Short Pie Crust Dough

MAKES 1 9-INCH UNBAKED PIE CRUST

This short pie crust dough is lighter and crispier than the Flaky Pie Crust Dough (page 194).

12 tablespoons (1½ sticks) unsalted
   butter, softened
¼ cup plus 2 tablespoons sugar
1 large egg yolk

¼ teaspoon grated orange zest
½ teaspoon vanilla extract
1½ cups all-purpose flour
¼ teaspoon table salt

Using a handheld mixer or stand mixer fitted with the flat beater attachment, beat the butter and sugar on medium speed until fluffy, scraping the bowl once or twice while mixing. Add the egg yolk, orange zest, and vanilla, and mix on medium speed until blended. Scrape the bowl and add the flour and salt, mixing on low speed until fully incorporated. When the dough resembles a stiff sugar dough, scrape it out onto a sheet of plastic wrap. Form the dough into a disk and refrigerate for at least 1 hour.

To roll out the dough, unwrap it and use the plastic wrap as the bottom surface. Place another large sheet of plastic on top of the dough. Roll the dough from the center into a 12-inch circle, flipping it (including the plastic) once or twice while rolling. With each flip, lift the plastic wrap from the surface of the dough to let the dough stretch, and then lay it back on the dough. When finished, lift the top piece of plastic off the dough. Invert the dough, holding it from the underside with the remaining plastic, into a 9-inch pie pan. Gently press the dough to mold it to the shape of the pan. Peel the plastic wrap off the dough.

Trim the edges, leaving ½ inch of dough overhanging. Fold the overhang under and crimp the edges to form a decorative rim. Chill until ready to use, up to 2 days.

hazelnuts

Take a drive through the lush Willamette Valley in Oregon and you're in filbert country. Row after row of bushy green trees hold promise of the rich nuts to come. You might hear a farmer say that "hazelnuts grow on filbert trees," recognizing that the nuts are called hazelnuts for marketing reasons but are known locally as filberts. Home to the largest hazelnut processor in the United States, Oregon is proud of its signature nut, and the 150-mile-long region produces 99 percent of the country's crop. Farmers tend to their trees all year long, hoping the fall harvest is as abundant as expected. During harvest, beating the rain is the main priority, but the wind helps shake reluctant nuts from the tree. When the smooth, hard nuts fall, they are sucked up with a machine that is essentially a giant vacuum and then brought to the factory to be shelled, sorted, and readied for shipment. In the Pacific Northwest, hazelnuts show up in almost every dish imaginable, adding crunch to salads and soups, coating fish—and, of course, paired with chocolate in cakes, cookies, and tarts.

While peeling hazelnuts can test the patience of even the most devoted cook, the resulting fragrant, buttery taste is worth the effort. Roasting hazelnuts in the oven and then rubbing them in a towel is the best method for removing the skins. It's impossible to remove 100 percent of the somewhat bitter skins, but a small amount of skin won't compromise a dish. The best technique is to purchase blanched hazelnuts, but they can be difficult to find.

Hazelnuts are sold whole, plain, or roasted, as well as chopped or ground into meal. Dry-roasted nuts, best kept in the refrigerator, can be used for up to one year. They can be frozen for up to two years. Hazelnut oil is a wonderful flavoring oil for soups and salads; it is typically imported from France.

PEAR-GINGER PIE

MAKES 1 9-INCH PIE

THE WASHINGTON STATE CLIMATE IS IDEAL for pear trees, and year-round our local markets stock endless varieties, such as sweet Anjou, aromatic Bosc, sweet and juicy Yellow Bartlett, and the crisp Comice. Pear and ginger play off each other in an interesting way, with the heat of ginger cutting the sweetness of the fruit. Be sure to use slightly underripe fruit for the best texture; overripe fruit has too much moisture for this pie.

Flaky Pie Crust Dough (recipe follows)
1 cup sugar
$1/3$ cup plus 2 tablespoons all-purpose flour
$1^{1}/_{4}$ teaspoons grated lemon zest
2 pinches of table salt
$1/3$ cup unsalted butter (about 5 tablespoons)

3 pounds pears, a mix of Anjou and Bartlett, peeled, cored, and thinly sliced (about 6 small pears)
$1/2$ teaspoon ground ginger
2 tablespoons minced crystallized ginger
2 tablespoons currants or raisins

To make the topping, in a small bowl, combine $1/2$ cup sugar, $1/3$ cup flour, $1/4$ teaspoon lemon zest, and 1 pinch of salt. Cut in the butter with a pastry blender or large fork until the mixture resembles coarse crumbs. Set aside until ready to use.

Position a rack in the lower third of the oven and preheat the oven to 400°F.

In a large bowl, combine the pears, remaining sugar, remaining flour, remaining lemon zest, the ground and crystallized ginger, the currants, and 1 pinch of salt. Pour into the prepared pie crust and sprinkle evenly with the topping.

Place the pie on a rimmed baking sheet to catch any drips. Bake for 15 minutes, reduce the oven temperature to 350°F., and continue to bake for 45 minutes, or until the filling is bubbly around the edges, the crust is golden, and the center of the pie is tender when pierced with a knife.

Cool to room temperature before slicing and serving.

MAKE AHEAD Cover and refrigerate the pie for up to 5 days.

Flaky Pie Crust Dough

MAKES 1 9-INCH PIE SHELL

The secret to a flaky crust is keeping the dough cold and rolling it between two sheets of plastic wrap. Do not roll the dough on a floured surface because that only incorporates more flour, pressing it into the butter and reducing the flakiness of the crust.

1½ cups all-purpose flour

½ teaspoon table salt

9 tablespoons cold unsalted butter, cut into pieces

In a large bowl, combine the flour and salt. Using a pastry blender or fork, cut in the butter until the mixture is coarse and crumbly. Sprinkle 3 to 4 tablespoons water over the mixture 1 tablespoon at a time while stirring the mixture with a fork. Add enough water to make the dough cohesive. Gently gather the dough with your hands and pat it firmly into a ball. (This dough is best when rolled out immediately.)

To roll out the dough, press it into a 7-inch circle on a sheet of plastic wrap. Place another large sheet of plastic wrap on top of the dough. Roll the dough from the center into a 12-inch circle, flipping the dough (including the plastic) once or twice while rolling. With each flip, lift the plastic wrap from the surface of the dough to let the dough stretch, and then lay it back on the dough. When finished, lift the top piece of plastic wrap off the dough. Invert the dough, holding it from the underside with the remaining plastic wrap, into a 9-inch pie pan. Gently press the dough to mold it to the shape of the pan. Peel the plastic wrap off the dough.

Trim the edges, leaving ½ inch of dough overhanging. Fold the overhanging dough under and crimp the edges to form a decorative rim. Chill until ready to use.

TOASTING NUTS

Using the oven to toast nuts is best. You get more uniformly toasted nuts than in a skillet on the stove, and there's less chance of burning them (if you set a timer, that is). Let toasted nuts cool completely before using them in a recipe or storing in an airtight container.

Almonds, Walnuts, and Pecans

Preheat the oven to 350°F.

Place the nuts on a baking sheet. Bake for 6 to 8 minutes, being careful not to burn the nuts. As the nuts toast, they will become fragrant and turn light brown.

Hazelnuts

Blanched hazelnuts are ideal, but they can be hard to find. The skin on whole hazelnuts can be a little bitter, so try to remove as much of it as possible. This is easier to do when the nuts are warm, because the skin blisters and cracks in the oven.

Preheat the oven to 350°F.

Place hazelnuts on a baking sheet. Bake for 15 minutes.

As the hazelnuts toast, they will become fragrant and the skins will crack and flake off. Pour the toasted nuts into the center of a clean kitchen towel, bring up the sides of the towel, and twist it closed to seal in the nuts. Rub the nuts together in the towel to remove as much of the brown skin as possible. (Don't bother trying to remove the skin from each individual hazelnut; it's virtually impossible.) Open the towel on a flat surface and gently roll the nuts away from the skins. Discard the skins.

cherries

Juicy sweet cherries are so prevalent in the Pacific Northwest that they're often taken for granted. They arrive in early summer and keep coming until late August, and unlike some other fruit, they never taste as good as they do in the heart of summer. Deep red, vivid yellow, or pale white, cherries are the epitome of the Northwest fruit harvest. There are seven major types, including the familiar sweet Bing and the blushing Rainier, but firm Lapins, the dark red Skeena, and the bright red Sweetheart varieties offer diversity of flavor. And while Washington State cherries are the best known, Utah, Oregon, and Idaho contribute their fair share of the crop. People from Michigan and New York State love their sour cherries, but we Pacific Northwesterners snack on the sweet varieties.

Fresh cherries add a zing to salads and brandied cherries add a deep note to both meats and desserts, but sometimes simple is best: A bowl of fresh cherries is a welcome sight on any table. Look for firm, taut, heavy, deeply colored fruit. An inexpensive cherry pitter makes pitting easy work. A glass of sweet red cherry juice is another way to enjoy cherries.

Baking with fresh cherries is often disappointing, as fresh cherries lose much of their flavor when baked. Many recipes add cherry extract to boost the flavor, but using dried cherries, both sweet and sour varieties, is a more flavorful, and healthier, option. Refrigerate your cherries and they will last for a few days—if they aren't devoured the instant you bring them home.

MOCHA–BUTTER CRUNCH PIE

MAKES 1 9-INCH ROUND PIE

WITH A CHOCOLATE CRUST and a creamy espresso filling, this pie is like a mocha cappuccino disguised as dessert. Here are a few tricks for a successful pie: Make sure the butter and cream for the filling are at room temperature, and remember to scrape the sides of the bowl frequently as you mix. For serving, cut the pie with a knife that's been dipped in hot water and wiped dry.

CHOCOLATE CRUST
1 cup all-purpose flour
2 tablespoons cocoa powder
2 tablespoons granulated sugar
1/4 cup powdered sugar
1/2 teaspoon table salt
6 tablespoons (3/4 stick) cold unsalted
    butter, cut into 6 pieces
1/2 cup walnuts, roughly chopped
2 teaspoons vanilla extract

FILLING
3 1/2 ounces bittersweet chocolate,
    chopped into 1/2-inch pieces
1 cup (2 sticks) unsalted butter, at room
    temperature
2 teaspoons instant espresso powder
2 1/2 teaspoons vanilla extract
1 cup sugar
1/2 cup heavy cream, at room temperature

TOPPING
1 1/2 cups heavy cream
2 teaspoons vanilla extract
1/3 to 1/2 cup powdered sugar

Preheat the oven to 350°F.

To make the crust, use a food processor to combine the flour, cocoa powder, granulated sugar, powdered sugar, and salt. Add the butter and pulse until it is cut into the dry mixture and the mixture looks like coarse meal. Transfer the mixture to a medium bowl and add the walnuts. In a separate bowl, combine the vanilla and 2 teaspoons water.

Stir the dry mixture while adding the vanilla and water until evenly moistened. If the dough is dry, add another 1 to 2 teaspoons of water, as needed. When it is finished, the dough will look crumbly but should hold together when squeezed lightly with your fingers. Spread an even layer of the mixture in the bottom of a 9-inch springform pan or cake pan with a removable bottom. Lay a sheet of plastic wrap over the mixture and, using your hands, press the crust evenly into the bottom of the pan and up the sides of the pan to a height of 1 1/4 to 1 1/2 inches. The crust on the bottom of the pan should be about 1/8 inch thick. (You might not use all of the mixture.)

Bake the crust for 20 to 25 minutes, or until it is dry and fragrant. Set aside and let cool to room temperature. Chill the crust until ready to use.

While the crust is baking, begin preparing the filling by melting the chocolate. First, place the chocolate pieces in a medium metal bowl. Then fill a medium saucepan with 1 inch hot water and heat over medium-low heat. Finally, place the metal bowl on top of the saucepan and melt the chocolate, stirring occasionally. (Alternatively, you can melt the mixture in a double boiler or in a microwave-safe bowl in the microwave in 15-second spurts.) Once the chocolate is melted, remove it from the heat.

Put the butter in the bowl of an electric mixer fitted with the wire whip attachment. (You could also use a handheld mixer.) Whip the butter on medium-high until it is light and fluffy, about 2 minutes, scraping the bowl once or twice while mixing.

In a separate bowl, dissolve the espresso powder into the vanilla. Add the sugar and the coffee mixture to the butter and beat for 2 minutes on medium-high. Pour in the melted chocolate and continue to mix for 2 minutes, scraping the bowl once or twice while mixing.

With the machine running, slowly pour the cream into the butter mixture. Continue to whip the mixture until thoroughly combined, scraping the bowl once or twice while mixing. Spread the mixture into the cooled shell. (If the shell is still warm, it will melt the chocolate mixture.)

Cover the pie with plastic wrap and refrigerate for at least 3 hours or overnight.

After the pie is chilled, make the topping by whipping the cream in the bowl of an electric mixer fitted with the wire whip attachment, or use a handheld mixer. Whip until soft peaks form. Add the vanilla and ⅓ cup powdered sugar and whip until thoroughly combined, about 30 seconds. Taste for sweetness and whip in more powdered sugar if desired. Spread the topping on the pie just before serving. Remove the ring from the pan, keeping the pie on the flat piece. Use a warm knife to slice the pie.

MAKE AHEAD The pie will keep, covered, for up to 5 days in the refrigerator. Add the topping just before serving.

Sally Jackson

Before there was any such thing as artisanal cheese on the American culinary scene, there was Sally Jackson. Starting out in her farm kitchen in eastern Washington State in 1974, Sally was one of the first to create handmade cheeses from goat's, cow's, and sheep's milk. These would eventually become some of the top artisanal cheeses in the country.

Sally's career as a cheesemaker came purely from her love of cheese. "My husband Roger and I moved to Washington State with three kids, a cow, and two goats," says Sally. "I started fooling around with making cheese when the kids were little. People tasted it and they liked it, and as we got more animals and I had more time, I made more and more cheese." After reading about sheep's-milk cheeses, Sally bought two sheep and gave it a try. Soon she and Roger were selling the cheese at the local commune, with locals lining up in the town parking lot to buy her cheese, butter, and ice cream. "It was the first marketing we did," notes Sally.

After local success, Sally and Roger drove to Seattle to meet with restaurants, hotels, and grocery stores in the city. They quickly established a customer base and, without further marketing effort, developed nonstop demand for her wheels of cheese, wrapped in grape leaves or chestnut leaves grown in a local orchard. Sally still makes everything by hand and is loyal to her state. "I don't believe in sending all of my cheese too far away," says Sally. "I like the idea of having it local." Fortunately for cheese lovers everywhere, Sally's handcrafted cheeses can be found at specialty markets throughout the United States, and there's no question that it's worth the small effort to seek them out.

HONEY BLANK SLATE CHEESECAKE

MAKES 1 8-INCH ROUND CHEESECAKE

THIS CREAMY CHEESECAKE IS MUCH LIGHTER THAN the classic New York cheesecake. Instead of cream cheese, we use Beecher's Honey Blank Slate, a naturally cultured, soft, fresh farmer's cheese blended with Washington State honey, but a good substitute is fresh ricotta cheese mixed with honey. One tip for a successful cheesecake: Before serving, run a knife around the edge to separate it from the pan. This will help prevent the cheesecake from cracking. Top the cheesecake with Caramel Sauce (page 183) or Northwest Berry Syrup (page 221).

1 cup graham cracker crumbs	$1/2$ teaspoon grated lemon zest
5 tablespoons unsalted butter, melted	2 teaspoons orange liqueur or rum
16 ounces ricotta cheese	Pinch of table salt
6 tablespoons honey	2 large eggs, separated
$1^1/4$ teaspoons vanilla extract	2 teaspoons all-purpose flour

Center a rack in the oven and preheat the oven to 350°F.

To make the crust, in a medium bowl, combine the cracker crumbs and butter, mixing thoroughly. Press the crumb mixture into the bottom of an 8-inch springform pan. Bake for 15 minutes, or until golden. Let the crust cool while you prepare the filling. Leave the oven on.

Using a food processor, blend the ricotta, honey, vanilla, lemon zest, orange liqueur, and salt for 30 seconds, scraping the sides of the bowl. Add the egg yolks and flour. Pulse for 30 seconds until smooth. Scrape the sides of the bowl and transfer the mixture into a medium bowl.

Using a handheld or stand mixer fitted with the whisk attachment, beat the egg whites until stiff peaks form. Fold the egg whites gently into the cheese mixture. Pour the mixture into the prepared crust and bake until the edges are slightly puffed and the center jiggles slightly, about 30 minutes.

Let the cheesecake cool for 5 minutes and then run a knife carefully around the edge of the cake to loosen it from the pan. Cool the cheesecake for an additional 45 minutes and then refrigerate until ready to serve.

MAKE AHEAD The cheesecake will keep, covered, for up to 5 days in the refrigerator.

THE CHEESE PLATE

A cheese plate should be not only a culinary experience but also a conversation starter. Every artisanal cheese comes with a story: where it's from, the type of animal's milk used, and the people who made it. A well-designed cheese plate has a theme, either one of similarity or a theme of difference that makes the tasting even more interesting. Arrange the cheese plate according to a region, a type of cheese, or around a trip to your favorite cheese shop or cheesemaker in your area. (Farmer's markets are a great place to sample local cheeses.)

Three types of cheese on one platter are plenty; any more can be overwhelming for both the palate and the stomach. A great starter plate includes a piece of aged Cheddar, a blue-veined cheese, and a bloomy or washed rind, such as Brie or Muenster. Other possible combinations include one cheese each of cow's, goat's, and sheep's milk, or three different cheeses from Italy, such as Gorgonzola, Parmigiano-Reggiano, and Tallegio. Serving three different Cheddars is a great way to experience the differences in one style of cheese, and offering three different ages of the same cheese is an interesting way to taste how cheese matures.

Cheese should be served at the same temperature as red wine, about 65°F. Cheese gets flat at room temperature, but similarly it shouldn't be ice cold, either, as you won't experience its full flavor. Store your cheese in the refrigerator until a half-hour before serving. This differs from what many cheese books suggest, but I find this method produces the best combination of texture and flavor. Any cheese with a molded rind should not be wrapped in plastic. Instead, wrap it loosely in waxed paper.

A wooden cheese board is ideal for serving, and cheese knives make cutting the cheese an easy task. (The knives with holes in them are the best because they cut through both soft and hard cheeses easily.) In France, cheese is traditionally served before dessert, but I prefer to eat my cheese as an appetizer. Party guests can nibble on the cheese while everyone's arriving, and it's a great way to set the mood.

Whether you prefer eating your cheese with or without bread, a basket of good crackers and plain artisanal bread is a delicious way to round out a cheese plate. And get creative with accompaniments: Thai chile sauce pairs wonderfully with Brie, and quince paste goes well with hard aged cheeses. A handful of salted nuts make a great palate cleanser.

Teaching wine and cheese pairing classes has shown me that you can make a mediocre wine taste better with cheese but you can also ruin a great cheese with bad wine. Don't splurge on the cheese and then serve inferior wine, or the difference will be glaring. Cheeses and wines vary so greatly when it comes to flavor that suggesting specific pairings is haphazard at best. In general, goat cheese pairs well with white wine and, at the other end of the spectrum, super-stinky blues are great with fortified wines. Experiment and see what tastes best to you. Always remember that no one is the expert on anyone else's palate.

BREAKFAST

FRUIT SALAD WITH VANILLA SYRUP

THE BIG OMELET

BREAKFAST STRATA

CORN, TOMATO, AND AVOCADO FRITTATA

POACHED EGGS WITH CHEESE SAUCE

LATKES

MASA FLOUR PANCAKES WITH THREE-CITRUS
HONEY-BUTTER SYRUP

APPLE-HAZELNUT WAFFLES WITH NORTHWEST BERRY SYRUP

BLUEBERRY BUCKLE

DEEP-DISH CINNAMON BUNS

DECADENT HOT CHOCOLATE

FRUIT SALAD
with Vanilla Syrup

SERVES 6

FRUIT SALADS ARE BEST when based on what's in season. While the fruit may change, I always use a delicious vanilla syrup that works wonders with any combination. Below is a list of what fruits you'll find in season that pair well in this salad.

6 tablespoons sugar

1/4 teaspoon ground cinnamon

Pinch of freshly ground black pepper

1 tablespoon freshly squeezed lemon juice

1 1/2 teaspoons vanilla extract

6 cups cubed fruit

Combine 1 cup water with the sugar, cinnamon, and pepper in a small saucepan. Bring to a boil over high heat, lower the heat, and simmer until the sugar is dissolved, about 2 minutes.

Remove the syrup from the heat and stir in the lemon juice and vanilla. Let cool to room temperature before using.

Toss the fruit with the syrup and serve.

MAKE AHEAD The syrup can be stored in a covered container in the refrigerator for up to 1 week.

SEASONAL FRUIT

WINTER	SPRING	SUMMER	FALL	YEAR-ROUND
Apples, such as Gala, Fuji, Braeburn	Apples, such as Gala, Fuji, Braeburn	Apricots	Apples, such as Gala	Apples, such as Red Delicious, Golden Delicious, Granny Smith
Grapefruit	Apricots	Blueberries	Grapes	Bananas
Kiwi	Berries	Cherries	Mandarin oranges	
Mandarin oranges	Grapes	Grapes	Pears, such as Bartlett	
Navel oranges	Kiwi	Mangoes	Pomegranates	
Papayas	Mangoes	Melons		
Pears, such as Bartlett, Bosc, d'Anjou, Red d'Anjou	Papayas	Nectarines		
	Pears, such as Bartlett, Bosc, d'Anjou	Peaches		
	Pineapple	Pineapples		
	Strawberries	Strawberries		
	Sweet oranges	Watermelon		

coffee

Coffee—the drink that Seattle made famous—is the breakfast of choice for many people. But there's more to coffee than "decaf or regular" (or even "black or half-caf mocha macchiato with skim"). How and where the beans are grown determines flavor. Here are some explanations of common coffee terms to help you choose an environmentally friendly cup of joe with maximum flavor.

ESTATE GROWN: Estate coffees come from a single estate or farm and are labeled with the name of that farm or grower as well as the region. (In contrast, a blend can be made up of two or more estate coffees.) Think of these as fine vintage wines from a single estate as opposed to less expensive blends.

CERTIFIED ORGANIC COFFEE: These beans are grown without the use of pesticides, and their growing conditions and processing are thoroughly monitored by independent agencies. This monitoring is an additional expense for the grower, which is why organic coffee can cost more.

FAIR TRADE: The Fair Trade Certified label guarantees a minimum wage for small farmers, who are often otherwise forced to work below market at the poverty level. It also guarantees eco-friendly practices that support sustainable agriculture. Most fair trade coffees are also organic. Farmers must pay to be certified by the nonprofit group Transfair USA, however, and not every farmer participates, even though he may be following the Fair Trade requirements.

SHADE GROWN: Coffee grown in heavily shaded areas, which in many cases decreases the need for chemicals, is sometimes labeled as such. Shade-grown coffees are beneficial to the environment, but the method does not guarantee better quality than non-shade-grown coffee.

SUSTAINABLE: This coffee designation is used by farmers who avoid agricultural chemicals and participate in responsible environmental practices in the growing and processing of their coffees. Because this type of farming is a voluntary commitment, with no regulating body, "sustainable" is not a certified or regulated term. It includes farmers in countries who have been farming coffee for centuries without chemicals and continue to do so but cannot afford the certification process for an organic label.

Most coffees include one or more of these labels, and they are not mutually exclusive. An estate coffee can be shade grown, sustainable, and organic. The estate category refers to *where* the coffee was grown, while the other categories refer to *how* the beans are grown or harvested. Only *certified organic* and *fair trade* are regulated designations; the rest are self-assigned. Purchasing certified organic coffee is your best option if you want to avoid chemicals and additives in your coffee, but shade-grown coffee is also beneficial to the environment.

DECAFFEINATED COFFEE: Contrary to common belief, caffeine is a crystalline substance that has no aroma and only a slightly bitter taste. This taste is lost in the other aromas of coffee, so decaffeinated coffee isn't less flavorful than regular coffee simply because it lacks caffeine.

Coffee is decaffeinated while the beans are in their green, or unroasted, state. There are three methods used to remove caffeine from coffee beans, the most common employing chemicals like methylene chloride or ethyl acetate. While methylene chloride has not been directly linked to any cancer by the National Cancer Institute, it is also used in products such as nail polish remover, and concerns about the effects on humans exist. Ethyl acetate is derived from fruit, so some coffee companies that use it label their coffee as "naturally decaffeinated." With both compounds, the beans are soaked in a caffeine-absorbing solvent, the caffeine is removed from the solvent, and then the process is repeated until sufficient caffeine is removed from the beans.

The second method doesn't involve chemicals. The Swiss Water® Process removes caffeine from the beans using only water by percolation through activated charcoal, without any added chemicals. (Water alone cannot be used because it removes too much flavor from the beans.) Look for "Swiss Water Process" on the label if you want to be sure your decaf coffee is chemical-free.

The third, least common method is the carbon dioxide method, where the beans are soaked in compressed carbon dioxide and the solvent containing the caffeine evaporates. This is a natural process with no harmful side effects.

Other than the Swiss Water Process, the decaffeination method used is rarely, if ever, indicated on the coffee label.

THE BIG OMELET

SERVES 4 TO 6

WHILE YOU USUALLY HAVE TO MAKE SEPARATE OMELETS for each person, with this recipe you can make one big omelet to feed the crowd. Fill it with whatever leftovers are found in the refrigerator; see the suggestions below.

8 large eggs

$\frac{1}{4}$ teaspoon kosher salt

5 grinds of freshly ground black pepper

Dash of Tabasco or other hot sauce

1 tablespoon unsalted butter

2 cups filling (examples follow)

4 ounces semihard grating cheese (page 23), grated (1 cup)

2 cups garnish (examples follow)

Place the top rack 4 inches from the top of the oven and preheat the broiler.

Whisk together the eggs, $\frac{1}{4}$ cup water, salt, pepper, and Tabasco sauce. Set aside.

Heat a 14-inch ovenproof skillet over medium-high heat and melt the butter. As the butter melts, rotate the skillet so the butter covers the bottom and sides. Pour in the egg mixture and rotate the skillet until the egg mixture covers the bottom of the pan. Cook for 3 minutes, or until the egg mixture is cooked halfway through, breaking any bubbles that form.

Transfer the skillet to the broiler, leaving the oven door open. Cook for 1 to 2 minutes, or until the center of the top of the omelet puffs up and begins to brown and the eggs are cooked. Remove the pan from the broiler. Leaving the omelet in the skillet, lay the filling on one half of the omelet and sprinkle all but 2 teaspoons of the cheese over the top.

Place the omelet back under the broiler and cook for 30 seconds, or until the cheese is melted. Remove from the oven and turn off the broiler. Using a spatula, loosen the edges of the omelet and fold the remaining half of the omelet over the filling. Slide the omelet onto a serving platter and top with the remaining cheese and the garnish.

MEDITERRANEAN OMELET
FILLING: Poached Chicken (page 230), Artichoke Spread (page 238)
GARNISH: Roasted Red Pepper Spread (page 236), chopped fresh flat-leaf parsley

GAME DAY OMELET
FILLING: Sliced Grilled Pork Blade Steak (page 124), Roasted Autumn Vegetables (page 149)
GARNISH: Dollop of sour cream, chopped fresh flat-leaf parsley

CRAB LOVER'S OMELET
FILLING: Leftover Crab Cake (page 78), drizzle of Lime Jalapeño Dressing (page 53)
GARNISH: Tangy Rémoulade (page 80)

LATKES

MAKES 8 4-INCH LATKES

LIGHT ENOUGH TO BE SERVED AS a casual breakfast dish but hearty enough to accompany a New York steak, these latkes have a crunchy, savory flavor due to two techniques: First, the potatoes are salted to remove most of the excess moisture and then browned in olive oil and butter for a rich, round flavor.

2 large russet potatoes, shredded

2 teaspoons kosher salt

2 teaspoons freshly squeezed lime juice

Freshly ground black pepper to taste

3 green onions (white and green parts), chopped

1 large shallot, chopped

2 tablespoons chopped fresh flat-leaf parsley

$1/2$ teaspoon Old Bay Seasoning

1 ounce semihard cheese (page 23), grated ($1/4$ cup)

$1/2$ cup toasted or dried bread crumbs

2 large eggs, beaten

4 tablespoons ($1/2$ stick) unsalted butter

4 tablespoons extra-virgin olive oil

Combine the potato, salt, and lime juice in a medium bowl and let sit for 5 minutes. Squeeze the potatoes between your hands to remove any liquid and transfer to a plate.

Dry the bowl and return the potato to it. Add the pepper, green onions, shallot, parsley, Old Bay, cheese, bread crumbs, and eggs. Using your hands, combine thoroughly.

In a large skillet over medium heat, heat 2 tablespoons of the butter and 2 tablespoons of the olive oil. Add $1/2$ cup of the potato mixture and spread it out to form a 4-inch pancake. Cook 4 latkes in the skillet at one time until golden brown, about 4 minutes. Using your spatula to loosen the latkes from the skillet, turn them over, and cook for 3 to 5 more minutes, or until they are golden brown. Remove to a serving plate. Add 2 tablespoons butter and 2 tablespoons olive oil to the skillet before cooking the second batch.

Serve warm.

MAKE AHEAD The latkes will keep, covered, in the refrigerator for up to 5 days. Reheat them slowly in a dry skillet over low heat.

MASA FLOUR PANCAKES
with Three-Citrus Honey-Butter Syrup

MAKES 8 4-INCH PANCAKES

A STACK OF FLUFFY, HOT PANCAKES can lure even the most dedicated sleeper out of bed. Made with masa flour (corn flour), these gluten-free pancakes have a decidedly corn flavor that is even better topped with a warm citrus honey-butter syrup or Northwest Berry Syrup (page 221). Masa flour, also known as masa harina, is available in most grocery stores and is commonly used in Mexican cooking.

2 teaspoons unpacked light brown sugar	1/4 teaspoon vanilla extract
1 to 1 1/2 cups masa flour	2 cups milk
2 1/2 teaspoons baking powder	1 tablespoon unsalted butter, melted
1/4 teaspoon table salt	Three-Citrus Honey-Butter Syrup (recipe
1 tablespoon salsa verde (mild to medium)	follows)
1 large egg	

In a large bowl, combine the brown sugar, 1 cup of the flour, the baking powder, and the salt. Set aside.

In a small bowl, whisk together the salsa verde, egg, vanilla, and milk. Slowly add the melted butter.

Gently stir the liquid mixture into the dry mixture until it is fully combined. The batter should be slightly thick. If it is not thick enough, add the remaining 1/2 cup flour. Let the batter sit for 5 minutes.

Heat a large nonstick griddle or nonstick skillet over medium heat. Pour 1/4 cup of the batter for each pancake onto the griddle, leaving 2 inches between the pancakes. When small bubbles form around the edges of the pancakes, at about 1 1/2 minutes, flip them with a spatula. (Corn flour pancakes have less structure than wheat flour pancakes, so be careful when flipping them.) The pancakes should be golden brown on the bottom. Cook for 1 additional minute, or until the bottom is golden brown.

Repeat with the remaining batter, keeping pancakes warm on an ovenproof plate in a 200°F. oven. Serve warm with Three-Citrus Honey-Butter Syrup.

Three-Citrus Honey-Butter Syrup

MAKES 1¹/₂ CUPS

Instead of pouring syrup and butter over a stack of pancakes, we put the butter in the syrup. This sweet and creamy syrup is also great on Cinnamon Buns (page 225).

2 teaspoons cornstarch

8 tablespoons (1 stick) unsalted butter

2 teaspoons grated orange zest

2 teaspoons grated lime zest

2 teaspoons grated grapefruit zest

¹/₂ cup freshly squeezed grapefruit juice

¹/₂ cup honey

Combine the cornstarch and 2 teaspoons water in a small bowl. Stir until the cornstarch is dissolved.

In a small saucepan over medium heat, melt the butter. Add the orange zest, lime zest, grapefruit zest, grapefruit juice, and honey. Bring to a boil and stir in the cornstarch mixture. Remove from the heat. Serve warm.

MAKE AHEAD The syrup will keep, covered, for up to 1 week in the refrigerator.

pacific northwest berries

In the Northwest, fresh berries are a beacon of summer. Besides sweet strawberries, plump red raspberries, bright blue blueberries, and deep black blackberries, marionberries, loganberries, and huckleberries are summer treats. Locals are passionate about their berries and will argue for hours about which berry is really the best.

Marionberries are large, deep purple blackberries, a cross between Chehalem and Olallie-berry blackberries, and get their name from Marion County, Oregon. Grown throughout Oregon and Washington, these simultaneously sweet and tart berries are picked in July and August. With mild spring weather and cool summer evenings, Oregon grows 30 million pounds each year. Eat them by the handful or try them in a pie. They're often made into jam.

Blueberries from the Northwest are simply perfect. Eight types of blueberry thrive in the acidic Washington State soil, and more than twenty varieties come from Oregon. Summer is the time for harvest, when baskets of bright blue berries crowd the markets. But the best blue-berries are found at the dozens of u-pick-'em farms, where you can pick until your basket is full and your fingers are stained dark purple.

Sweet red strawberries grow in abundance in Oregon and Washington in June and July. Rainier, Totem, Shuskan, Hood, and Puget Beauty are a few of the local varieties that find their way into desserts and jams (although I like to eat them out of hand).

Loganberries come with a little bit of controversy; most people say they're a cross between a blackberry and a raspberry, while others say the berry is its own unique species. Regardless, this sweet, tart ruby-colored berry is beloved in the Northwest. Jams, sauces, and pies are where loganberries shine during their short July and August season. The Loganberry Festival is held at Greenbank Farm on Whidbey Island, Washington, every July, complete with a loganberry pie-eating contest. Whidbey embodies the spirit of the Northwest: striking natural beauty, unspoiled land, and a welcoming, laid-back attitude. The island motto is "Do Nothing Here"—which doesn't preclude the locals from spending hours picking wild berries.

Tiny huckleberries are the most prized of the berries because they're picked only in August and grow only in the wild. They perish quickly so they don't ship well, making them a local delicacy, but you can often find them frozen. Don't mistake them for blueberries; these deep purple berries have a thicker skin than blueberries and tiny, hard seeds. They taste best fresh, preferably straight from the bush. Head to Klickitat County in Washington State, by Trout Lake, for the best chance of finding fresh huckleberries; vendors line the roads and sell them by the buckets. They come at a price—sometimes more than $20 for a gallon of berries—but they're worth it. If you can't get fresh or frozen, substitute blueberries.

Store berries in a paper bag in the refrigerator, and don't wash them until you're ready to eat them; they will last for 2 to 3 days.

APPLE-HAZELNUT WAFFLES
with Northwest Berry Syrup

WITH A HANDFUL OF RICH HAZELNUTS and diced apples, these Pacific Northwest waffles make a hearty and tasty weekend breakfast dish. The whole wheat flour adds a deeper flavor and bonus nutrients. Once you taste these waffles, you'll never use a waffle mix again.

2 cups whole wheat flour

2 tablespoons baking powder

1/2 teaspoon table salt

2 cups buttermilk

2 teaspoons vanilla extract

3 large eggs, separated

2 tablespoons packed light brown sugar

6 tablespoons (3/4 stick) unsalted butter, melted and cooled slightly

1/4 cup finely chopped hazelnuts

1/4 sweet apple, such as Fuji, peeled and diced (about 1/3 cup)

Northwest Berry Syrup (recipe follows)

Whisk together the flour, baking powder, salt, buttermilk, vanilla, egg yolks, brown sugar, and butter until just combined. Gently fold the hazelnuts and apples into the batter. Do not overmix.

In a separate bowl, beat the egg whites until stiff peaks form. Gently fold the egg whites into the batter.

Cook the waffles in a waffle iron according to manufacturer's instructions. Top the waffles with berry syrup.

Northwest Berry Syrup

MAKES ABOUT 3 CUPS

A far cry from anything in a bottle, this intensely flavored syrup tastes great over waffles, pancakes, and even ice cream. You can use one type of berry or a combination of berries.

4 cups fresh or frozen unsweetened
berries, such as blueberries,
raspberries, and blackberries, and
hulled strawberries

1/2 cup sugar
1 teaspoon freshly squeezed lemon juice
1 1/2 teaspoons arrowroot (see Note)

Combine the berries, sugar, lemon juice, and 1 cup water in a medium saucepan. Bring to a boil over medium-high heat, stirring frequently.

In a small bowl, stir together the arrowroot with 1 tablespoon water. Add the arrowroot mixture to the berries and stir. Reduce the heat to low and cook for 10 minutes. Use a whisk to break up the berries, but do not crush them.

Remove the pan from the heat, cool the syrup for 1 to 2 minutes, and serve.

MAKE AHEAD The syrup will keep in an airtight container in the refrigerator for up to 1 week or frozen for up to 2 months. Reheat over low heat until warm.

NOTE To thicken the syrup, arrowroot is a better choice than cornstarch because arrowroot doesn't get chalky and has no distinguishing flavor. As with cornstarch, arrowroot should be dissolved in a cold liquid before whisking into a hot liquid. This mixture is called a slurry. Cornstarch breaks down if heated for an extended period but arrowroot doesn't, so sauces thickened with arrowroot reheat better and can be kept warm.

BLUEBERRY BUCKLE

A BUCKLE IS AN AMERICAN COFFEE CAKE, and this sweet and moist version is a nice departure from muffins. Use fresh, juicy blueberries in the summer for a true blueberry flavor.

TOPPING
- 1/3 cup all-purpose flour
- 1/3 cup sugar
- 1/4 teaspoon grated lemon zest
- Pinch of table salt
- 3 tablespoons cold unsalted butter

BUCKLE
- 8 tablespoons (1 stick) unsalted butter, softened
- 3/4 cup sugar
- 1/2 teaspoon vanilla extract
- 1/2 teaspoon grated lemon zest
- 1 large egg
- 2 cups all-purpose flour
- 2 teaspoons baking powder
- 1/2 teaspoon table salt
- 3/4 cup milk, at room temperature
- 2 cups fresh (only if in season) or frozen blueberries

Preheat the oven to 350°F. Grease a 9-inch round baking pan.

Make the topping by combining the flour, sugar, lemon zest, and salt in a small bowl. Using a fork, cut in the butter until the mixture resembles coarse crumbs. Set aside.

To make the buckle, use a handheld mixer or stand mixer fitted with the flat beater attachment. Beat the butter and sugar on medium speed until fluffy, scraping the bowl once or twice while mixing. Blend in the vanilla and lemon zest. Add the egg and mix on medium speed to combine, scraping the bowl once.

In a separate bowl, combine the flour, baking powder, and salt.

Add the milk and the flour mixture alternately to the butter mixture, beating until smooth on medium to low speed after each addition. Pour the batter into the prepared pan, top with the blueberries, and sprinkle with the topping.

Bake for 45 to 55 minutes, or until a toothpick comes out clean when inserted in the middle of the buckle.

MAKE AHEAD The buckle will keep, covered, in the refrigerator for up to 2 days. You can also wrap it in plastic wrap and freeze it for up to 1 month.

DEEP-DISH CINNAMON BUNS

MAKES 16 BUNS

THESE CINNAMON BUNS WERE INSPIRED BY the Magic Bakery Café on Whidbey Island, a small island north of Seattle, known for its handmade baked goods. Waking up to the aroma of freshly baked buns is guaranteed to start your weekend on the right note. Adding the potato to the dough results in a very light and moist bun. If you prefer your sugar later in the day, serve the buns as a dessert with Three-Citrus Honey-Butter Syrup (page 218) drizzled over the top.

1 medium russet potato, peeled and cut into ½-inch pieces
2 teaspoons active dry yeast
½ cup granulated sugar
1¾ teaspoons table salt
15 tablespoons unsalted butter, melted, divided

1 large egg
4½ to 5 cups all-purpose flour
2 cups unpacked light brown sugar
1 tablespoon plus 1 teaspoon ground cinnamon

Place the potato in a medium saucepan and cover with 2½ cups water. Bring to a boil and cook until the potato pieces are very tender, about 15 minutes. Drain the potatoes, reserving 1¼ cups liquid and the potato pieces in separate bowls.

Cool the potato liquid until it is lukewarm (110 to 115°F.). Add the yeast and let sit for 10 minutes.

Mash the potato pieces until smooth. Measure ½ cup mashed potato.

Using an electric mixer fitted with the paddle attachment, mix together the yeast mixture, mashed potato, granulated sugar, 1½ teaspoons of the salt, 6 tablespoons of the butter, and the egg. Mix on low for 15 seconds. Add 2 cups of the flour and mix on low speed until thoroughly blended, about 1 minute. Switch to the dough hook attachment. Add 2½ cups flour and knead at medium speed, adding more flour as needed to make a soft, elastic dough, about 10 minutes. Scrape the dough into a large plastic bag with enough room for the dough to expand 1½ times in size. Seal the bag and place it in the refrigerator to rise overnight.

Turn out the dough onto a lightly floured surface and knead it a few times to soften. Portion the dough into 16 equal pieces and roll each portion into a smooth ball.

Mix 8 tablespoons of the butter and the remaining ¼ teaspoon salt in a large, shallow bowl. Mix the brown sugar and cinnamon in a separate large, shallow bowl. Dip each bun in the butter, coating the entire surface, and then roll it in the brown sugar. Make sure there is plenty of the sugar and cinnamon mixture on each bun.

[RECIPE CONTINUES]

Using a pastry brush, grease a 9 x 13-inch baking dish with the remaining 1 tablespoon butter. Place the buns in the dish, cover them with a piece of oiled plastic wrap, and let them rise in a warm, draft-free space until they are 1½ times their original size, 45 minutes to 1 hour.

Preheat the oven to 350°F.

Bake the buns for about 25 minutes, or until they are light golden on top and a toothpick comes out clean when inserted in the middle of the center bun. Remove the buns from the oven and immediately turn them out onto a serving platter. Let the buns cool for at least 5 minutes.

To serve, cut apart the buns. Place each bun on a small plate and drizzle with the syrup from the bottom of the baking dish.

MAKE AHEAD You can prepare the buns in advance, freeze them, and reheat them. Let the buns cool, wrap them in plastic wrap, and freeze for up to 1 month. To reheat, unwrap the buns and bake them in a 350°F. oven for about 30 minutes.

DECADENT HOT CHOCOLATE

MAKES 4 CUPS

THIS IS TRUE HOT CHOCOLATE—as opposed to cocoa—made by melting chocolate into hot milk. It doesn't take any longer than hot cocoa to prepare but is a richer and creamier concoction. Top each mug with a dollop of whipped cream, marshmallows, or ground cinnamon, or dunk your favorite cookie into it.

4 cups milk
1/2 teaspoon vanilla extract
1/8 teaspoon kosher salt

4 to 6 ounces semisweet chocolate, finely chopped

Heat the milk in a medium saucepan over medium heat until it is just below simmering, stirring occasionally. Remove the pan from the heat and add the vanilla, salt, and chocolate to taste. Whisk the milk until the chocolate is completely melted. Reheat the milk gently over low heat, as needed.

Serve immediately.

BASICS, SAUCES & SPREADS

CHICKEN STOCK

MAKES 12 CUPS STOCK AND 1 POACHED CHICKEN

MAKING CHICKEN STOCK is one of the easiest things in the world; toss the ingredients in a pot and let it simmer while you do something else. After trying dozens of recipes, I settled on this one, which makes a pot of stock and a poached chicken for dinner or lunch the next day. Crunchy Chicken and Rice Salad (page 53), The Big Omelet (page 210), Chicken Salad with Corn and Cilantro (page 51), and Chicken-Avocado Salad (page 49) are delicious ways to enjoy the poached chicken. Browning the vegetables increases the flavor of the stock and lends a nice golden color. Adding wine enriches the flavor while deglazing the pan.

2 tablespoons unsalted butter
1 large yellow onion, unpeeled and
    quartered
2 carrots, roughly chopped

2 large celery ribs, roughly chopped
$1^{1}/_{2}$ cups white wine
1 whole chicken (about $3^{1}/_{2}$ to 4 pounds),
    giblets removed

In a 10-quart stockpot, melt the butter over medium heat. Add the onion, carrots, and celery. Increase the heat to medium-high and cook without stirring for 2 minutes while the vegetables caramelize.

Stir and continue to cook until the vegetables are browned, about 10 minutes. Add the wine, bring to a boil, and boil until the liquid is reduced by half, about 5 minutes. Add the chicken and 1 gallon cold water. Bring to a boil, reduce the heat to low, and simmer for 1 hour, skimming off any scum that forms on the surface.

After 1 hour, check the chicken for doneness. The chicken is done when the leg pulls away easily from the body or when a meat thermometer inserted into the thickest part of the meat, without touching the bone, reads 165°F. Remove the cooked chicken from the broth and set it aside until it is cool enough to handle, about 10 minutes, while keeping the stock at a simmer. Remove the meat from the bones, refrigerating the chicken meat for later use. Return the bones to the stock and simmer for another hour, skimming off any scum that forms on the surface.

Pour the stock through a fine-mesh strainer into a container, discarding the solids, and let cool to room temperature, about 30 minutes. Use the stock the same day it is made, or let it cool for 1 day in the refrigerator to skim the most fat from the stock. Pour the stock into containers and refrigerate overnight, uncovered. The next day, remove the fat that has formed on the top.

MAKE AHEAD Both the stock and the chicken
will keep for 5 days in the refrigerator or for up
to 6 months in the freezer. Store them separately.

TURKEY STOCK

Instead of waiting until Thanksgiving, I make turkey stock year-round, using turkey legs and wings. Just as versatile as chicken stock but with a decidedly different flavor, turkey stock is a wonderful addition to soups and sauces. Because this stock simmers for so long, the meat will not have any flavor left in it and should be discarded when the stock is ready.

Prepare Chicken Stock, opposite, substituting 10 pounds turkey wings and legs for the chicken. Do not remove the turkey after 1 hour; instead, simmer for a full 3 hours before straining and storing.

CRAB STOCK

MAKES 10 CUPS

YOU CAN'T BUY THIS INTENSELY FLAVORED STOCK anywhere; you have to make it yourself from fresh crab shells. In the Pacific Northwest there are two types of crab available, Dungeness and Alaska king crabs. We use Dungeness for its sweet crab flavor, but king crab can be substituted. We don't recommend using Atlantic blue crabs, as they have a completely different flavor. In my house, making the stock always comes the day after a crab feast. Crab stock is a wonderful base for any fish stew, but it plays the starring role in the Crab Mac and Cheese (page 74). Without it, the cheese overwhelms the flavorful crab.

$1/4$ cup extra-virgin olive oil
Shells of 3 crabs (medium-sized,
   $1^1/2$ pounds each), carapace (top shell)
   discarded

1 medium onion, roughly chopped
2 celery ribs, roughly chopped
1 cup white wine

Heat the oil in a 10-quart stockpot over high heat. Add the shells, onion, and celery and sauté for 10 minutes, or until the shells are lightly browned. Occasionally scrape the bottom of the pan while sautéing, as the shells may stick. Add the wine and cook for 4 to 5 minutes.

Add enough cold water to the pot to cover the shells. Bring to a boil, reduce the heat to low, and simmer for 1 hour, skimming off any scum that forms on the surface.

Pour the stock through a fine-mesh strainer into a shallow container, discarding the solids, and let cool to room temperature (about 30 minutes).

MAKE AHEAD The stock will keep for up to 5 days in the refrigerator or for up to 6 months in the freezer.

HOUSE HERBS

CREATED TWENTY YEARS AGO by Pasta & Co founder Marcella Rosene, this unique blend of dried herbs is exceptionally versatile.

2 tablespoons dried rosemary

1/4 cup dried oregano

1/4 cup dried basil

1/2 teaspoon allspice

1 tablespoon dried marjoram

1 1/2 tablespoons dried thyme

1 tablespoon freshly ground white pepper

2 tablespoons freshly ground black pepper

In a food processor, pulse the rosemary until it is finely chopped.

In a small bowl, mix together the rosemary, oregano, basil, allspice, marjoram, thyme, white pepper, and black pepper.

Store the herbs in an airtight container in a dry place. (Heat, bright light, and air destroy the flavor of herbs, and moisture can cause mold.) For best flavor, use within 6 months.

NOTE If you don't want to make a full cup of herbs, just reduce the quantity. To make 3 1/4 tablespoons House Herbs, combine 1 1/2 teaspoons rosemary, 1 tablespoon oregano, 1 tablespoon basil, a pinch of allspice, 3/4 teaspoon marjoram, 1 teaspoon thyme, 1/4 teaspoon white pepper, and 1/2 teaspoon black pepper.

BASIC MAYONNAISE

MAKES ABOUT 1 CUP

MAKING MAYONNAISE FROM SCRATCH is easy and worth the effort; the flavors are much more intense than in store-bought mayonnaise. If you don't have time to make your own, look for a brand that is free of hydrogenated oils. Mayonnaise easily takes on new flavors, and adding ingredients, such as pesto and wasabi, makes unusual and savory sandwich spreads and vegetable dips.

1 large egg yolk
1/4 teaspoon kosher salt
1/2 teaspoon Dijon mustard
1 1/2 teaspoons freshly squeezed lemon
   juice

1 teaspoon white wine vinegar
3/4 cup neutral-flavored cooking oil, such
   as canola or soybean

In a food processor or in a medium bowl, using a whisk, blend the egg yolk, salt, mustard, lemon juice, and white wine vinegar until the yolk thickens and the color brightens, about 20 seconds in a processor.

With the processor running or whisking constantly by hand, add the oil in a slow, steady stream. Process until the oil is fully absorbed into the egg, about 30 seconds in a processor.

MAKE AHEAD The mayonnaise will keep, covered, in the refrigerator for up to 3 days.

Southwest Mayonnaise

MAKES 2 CUPS

This spicy mayonnaise adds a kick to any sandwich.

1 7-ounce can chipotle chiles in adobo
sauce
4 garlic cloves
4 teaspoons firmly packed light brown
sugar

$1/2$ teaspoon kosher salt
1 tablespoon freshly squeezed lemon juice
1 cup Basic Mayonnaise (opposite) or any
all-natural mayonnaise
$1/2$ cup sour cream

In a food processor, puree the chiles to a smooth consistency. Set aside 3 tablespoons of the chipotle puree. (The chipotle chile puree can be spicy, so add less than the 3 tablespoons to reduce the heat in the mayonnaise.) The remaining puree can be frozen for another use.

Clean the bowl of the food processor and add the garlic and brown sugar. Pulse. Scrape down the sides of the work bowl and add the salt, lemon juice, mayonnaise, sour cream, and the reserved chipotle puree. Process to combine thoroughly.

MAKE AHEAD The mayonnaise will keep in an airtight container in the refrigerator for up to 3 days. If you are using store-bought mayonnaise, it can be stored for up to 1 month.

Pesto Mayonnaise

MAKES ABOUT 1 CUP

Try this mayonnaise on chicken or turkey sandwiches.

To 1 cup Basic Mayonnaise or any all-natural mayonnaise, add at least 3 tablespoons and up to $1/4$ cup store-bought or homemade pesto.

Wasabi Mayonnaise

MAKES ABOUT 1 CUP

Wasabi mayonnaise adds a kick to any sandwich. It tastes great with seafood, especially when it's mixed in a shrimp salad.

To 1 cup Basic Mayonnaise or any all-natural mayonnaise, add 1 to 2 teaspoons wasabi paste.

ROASTED RED PEPPER SPREAD

MAKES 1¹/₂ CUPS

THE SWEET, SMOKY FLAVORS of red peppers are accented with briny olives and feta for a savory spread. We prefer piquillo peppers, which aren't nearly as spicy as jalapeños but have a bit more heat than red bell peppers, but any jarred red pepper will do. Piquillo peppers are sold in jars and are available at most specialty stores. A perfect spread for artisanal breads and vegetables, it can also be served over grilled meats such as lamb or steak, added to The Big Omelet (page 210), or spooned over a green salad.

2 garlic cloves
2 tablespoons balsamic vinegar
1 tablespoon extra-virgin olive oil
1 red bell pepper, roasted
2 ounces jarred piquillo peppers (about 3 peppers; see Note)

12 kalamata olives, pitted
3 tablespoons roughly chopped fresh basil
¹/₄ teaspoon kosher salt
¹/₈ teaspoon freshly ground black pepper
1 ounce (about ¹/₄ cup) feta cheese

Using a food processor, puree the garlic with the balsamic vinegar and olive oil. Add the red bell pepper, piquillo peppers, olives, basil, salt, and pepper and pulse until the peppers and olives are finely chopped. Add the feta and pulse 4 to 6 times until the feta is incorporated but still coarse.

The spread can be refrigerated in an airtight container for up to 2 weeks.

NOTE For a sharper, more piquant flavor, substitute an additional 2 ounces piquillo peppers (about 3 peppers) for the red bell pepper. For a softer, sweeter spread, leave out the piquillo peppers and include 1 additional red bell pepper.

ARTICHOKE SPREAD

THIS CREAMY SPREAD can be used for breakfast, lunch, or dinner. It adds a tangy element to The Big Omelet (page 210), and spread on bread instead of mayonnaise, it dresses up any sandwich. For an easy appetizer, serve the spread on crostini or with a platter of fresh or grilled vegetables. Artichoke hearts are available in cans or jars, but we prefer canned because they're brined instead of marinated, lending a milder flavor to the spread. See photograph on page 237.

1 15-ounce can artichoke hearts

$^1/_2$ cup Basic Mayonnaise (page 234) or any all-natural mayonnaise

1 ounce hard grating cheese, such as Parmesan (page 23), grated ($^1/_4$ cup)

3 ounces semihard grating cheese (page 23), grated ($^3/_4$ cup)

1$^1/_2$ green onions (white and green parts), thinly sliced

$^1/_8$ teaspoon dried tarragon, crumbled

Pinch of cayenne pepper

$^1/_8$ teaspoon kosher salt

Dash of freshly ground black pepper

Drain the artichoke hearts and squeeze them to remove as much moisture as possible.

Using a food processor, pulse the artichoke hearts until finely chopped. Transfer them to a medium bowl and stir in the mayonnaise, hard cheese, semihard cheese, green onions, tarragon, cayenne, salt, and black pepper. Mix thoroughly.

Serve at room temperature or gently warmed in a saucepan over low heat.

MAKE AHEAD The spread will keep, covered, in the refrigerator for up to 5 days.

MOROCCAN OLIVE DIP

THIS RECIPE BEGAN AS A MARINADE for poached chicken, but it was so delicious we now sell it as a dip. Poured over a wedge of soft Brie cheese or served in a flat-bottomed bowl alongside bread, it makes an easy starter to any meal. A mix of golden and Thompson seedless raisins provides a sweet contrast. See photograph on page 237.

1 teaspoon ground cumin
1 teaspoon dried oregano
1 teaspoon fennel seeds
1¹/₄ teaspoons red pepper flakes
¹/₂ teaspoon dried rosemary, crushed
8 garlic cloves, crushed
2 cups pitted green olives, cut in half
  lengthwise

¹/₂ cup plus 2 tablespoons extra-virgin
  olive oil
¹/₄ cup freshly squeezed lemon juice
  (about 1 lemon)
1¹/₂ tablespoons red wine vinegar
1¹/₂ tablespoons sugar
³/₄ teaspoon kosher salt
Pinch of ground cloves
¹/₃ cup raisins

In a large covered container, combine the cumin, oregano, fennel seeds, 1 teaspoon of the red pepper flakes, and the rosemary, garlic, and olives. Add just enough water to cover the olives with liquid. Cover and let sit overnight in the refrigerator.

Strain the liquid from the olives and discard it. Pick out and discard the garlic. Add the olive oil, lemon juice, vinegar, sugar, salt, the remaining ¹/₄ teaspoon red pepper flakes, the cloves, and the raisins to the olives. Stir and then refrigerate for 1 hour.

Before serving, let the mixture sit at room temperature for 15 minutes to warm the olive oil. Stir and serve.

MAKE AHEAD The olive mixture will keep in an airtight container for up to 1 week in the refrigerator. Allow the mixture to come to room temperature before serving. (The oil may congeal while refrigerated.)

FRESH CRANBERRY SAUCE

MAKES 2³/₄ CUPS

EVERYONE HAS A FAVORITE cranberry sauce recipe, made once a year for Thanksgiving, but cranberry sauce is so versatile it really should be a year-round condiment. This is a longtime Pasta & Co favorite, where dried sour cherries add sweetness and depth to the tart cranberries. You can find sour cherries at specialty stores, often in the bulk food section.

1 12-ounce bag fresh cranberries, washed and dried

³/₄ cup dried sour cherries

³/₄ cup sugar

¹/₄ cup dark rum

In a large saucepan, combine the cranberries, sour cherries, sugar, and ¹/₂ cup water. Over medium-low heat, bring the mixture to a simmer and cook, stirring occasionally, about 5 to 7 minutes, or until the cranberries begin to pop. The cranberries should be tender but not mushy.

Remove the sauce from the heat and stir in the rum. Cool the sauce to room temperature and refrigerate it overnight to thicken. (You can eat the cranberry sauce the same day, once it cools to room temperature.) Bring the sauce to room temperature before serving.

MAKE AHEAD The sauce will keep, covered, in the refrigerator for up to 3 months.

MARINARA SAUCE
with Fresh Herbs

MAKES 4 CUPS

THIS IS OUR BASIC RED SAUCE and a recipe you will turn to again and again. It's one of the most versatile marinara sauces around, topping pasta, homemade pizza, or fresh seafood.

3 tablespoons extra-virgin olive oil
1 tablespoon minced garlic (3 cloves)
1/4 teaspoon red pepper flakes
2 cups white wine
1 28-ounce can crushed tomatoes or
    4 cups chopped fresh tomatoes

1 tablespoon chopped fresh basil
1 tablespoon chopped fresh oregano
1 teaspoon anchovy paste
Kosher salt to taste
1/2 teaspoon sugar (optional)

In a heavy 2-quart saucepan, heat the olive oil over medium heat and sauté the garlic and red pepper flakes for 1 to 2 minutes. Be careful not to brown the garlic. Add the wine and simmer for 10 to 12 minutes, or until the wine is reduced by half.

Reduce the heat to low, add the tomatoes, and simmer, partially covered, for 20 minutes, stirring occasionally. Add the basil, oregano, and anchovy paste. Stir the sauce and taste for seasoning, adding salt as needed. If the sauce is too acidic, add the sugar. (It will help round out the flavor of the sauce.) Stir and simmer the sauce for 1 to 2 minutes. For a thicker sauce, cook for an additional 10 minutes.

MAKE AHEAD The sauce will keep, covered, in the refrigerator for up to 7 days or in the freezer for up to 6 months.

TURKEY GRAVY
with Shallots and Mushrooms

MAKES 3 CUPS

NO THANKSGIVING TURKEY IS COMPLETE WITHOUT a richly flavored gravy, but this is so good you'll be using it year-round. Unlike most gravies, it can be made ahead to cut down on cooking stress.

8 cups Turkey Stock (page 231)

3 tablespoons unsalted butter

1/2 cup diced button or crimini mushrooms

3 tablespoons minced shallot

3 tablespoons plus 1 teaspoon all-purpose flour

1/4 teaspoon fresh thyme

3/4 teaspoon kosher salt

1/4 teaspoon freshly ground black pepper

In a large saucepan, reduce the turkey stock over medium-high heat to 3 cups. This will take about 30 minutes and will concentrate the turkey flavor. Set aside.

In a medium saucepan over medium-high heat, melt the butter. Add the mushrooms and shallots and cook for 3 minutes. Add the flour and cook for 2 minutes, whisking occasionally. Slowly add 1 cup of the reduced turkey stock and whisk until fully combined. Add the remaining stock, thyme, salt, and pepper. Whisk over medium heat for 3 to 5 minutes, or until thickened. Taste for seasoning and add salt and pepper, as needed.

MAKE AHEAD The gravy will keep, covered, in the refrigerator for up to 5 days. Reheat it gently over medium heat before serving.

HERBED CROUTONS

MAKES 8 CUPS

HOMEMADE CROUTONS ARE IN A CATEGORY all their own—boxed croutons just can't compete and are usually full of additives. Given leftover artisanal bread and a few herbs, nothing could be easier. Thrown in a salad or topping a soup, herbed croutons add a satisfying crunch to every dish. Even the most finicky kid will grab a handful to snack on.

$\frac{1}{2}$ cup extra-virgin olive oil
1 tablespoon finely minced garlic (about 3 cloves)

1 tablespoon House Herbs (page 233) or other Italian herb blend
24 ounces day-old bread, cut into $\frac{1}{2}$-inch cubes ($1\frac{1}{2}$ pound loaf)

Preheat the oven to 350°F.

In a large bowl, mix together the oil, garlic, and herbs. Add the bread and toss with the oil mixture until it is evenly coated.

Lay the bread on a baking sheet and bake for 10 minutes. Stir the croutons and bake for 10 more minutes. Continue cooking and stirring every 3 to 4 minutes until the croutons are toasted and golden. (Cooking time may vary.)

MAKE AHEAD The croutons will keep in an airtight container in a dry place. For best flavor, use within 3 weeks.

BREADZELS

THIS LONGTIME PASTA & CO FAVORITE crosses a pretzel with a breadstick. (The word *brezel* is German for "breadstick.") Flagship and Just Jack cheeses give the breadsticks a creamy flavor, but you can substitute Gruyère, Cheddar, or Parmesan. Don't let the thought of making dough intimidate you; it's easy to get the hang of and worth the effort. You can, however, use pre-made pizza dough; 2 pounds of dough will make 10 breadsticks.

DOUGH

1/4 cup warm water (110 to 115°F.)

3/4 teaspoon sugar

1 package active dry yeast

2 cups all-purpose flour

1 1/4 cups semolina flour

3/4 teaspoon kosher salt

7/8 cup cold water

2 1/2 tablespoons extra-virgin olive oil

TOPPING

1/2 cup extra-virgin olive oil

9 garlic cloves, minced

1 1/2 tablespoons dried basil

1 tablespoon dried oregano

2 teaspoons dried thyme

1 teaspoon kosher salt

1/2 teaspoon cayenne pepper

4 ounces semihard cheese (page 23), grated (1 cup)

4 ounces semisoft cheese (page 23), grated (1 cup)

For the dough, combine the warm water and sugar in a small bowl. Sprinkle the yeast over the top and let sit until foamy, about 10 minutes. Combine the flour, semolina, and salt in a large bowl. Stir in the yeast and then add the cold water and the olive oil. Mix to form a smooth and stiff (but not sticky) dough. Knead the dough in a stand mixer, a food processor, or by hand on a lightly floured board for about 5 minutes, or until smooth. Place the dough in a lightly oiled bowl, cover with a kitchen towel, and let it rise in a warm place for 1 hour, or until doubled in size.

For the topping, combine the olive oil, garlic, basil, oregano, thyme, salt, and cayenne in a small bowl and set aside. Combine the cheeses in another bowl and set aside.

Preheat the oven to 400°F. Line 2 baking sheets with parchment paper.

Divide the dough in 2 equal portions. Roll each piece into a 9 x 7-inch rectangle, using only as much extra flour as needed to keep the dough from sticking.

Spread the olive oil topping over the entire surface of each rectangle. Sprinkle each with half of the grated cheese. Press the cheese firmly into the dough with your fingers. Using a sharp knife, cut each rectangle of dough lengthwise into 5 equal strips.

Gently separate 1 strip, using a spatula if necessary. To twist the breadzels, lift half of the strip by placing one hand in the middle and the other at one end. Twist the end two complete revolutions away from you. Then lift the other half of the strip and twist it two complete revolutions toward you. Twist the whole breadzel one more time. (Some of the cheese will fall off during this process.) Lift the breadzel and place it on one of the prepared baking sheets, stretching it to about 13 inches in length. Repeat this process with the remaining strips, spacing them evenly on the baking sheet. Gather any cheese that fell off during the twisting process and gently press it back onto the dough. Cover with oiled plastic wrap and let rise in a warm place for 30 minutes.

Bake the breadzels for 15 minutes, or until golden brown. Remove the breadzels from the oven and let cool on the baking sheet for about 5 minutes, or until the melted cheese solidifies. Serve warm.

MAKE AHEAD Breadzels can be prepared ahead of time and frozen until you are ready to serve them. Par-bake them for 8 to 10 minutes and then let them cool before wrapping them in plastic wrap and freezing them. To serve, bake them in a 400°F. oven for 4 to 6 minutes, or until golden brown.

GREEN BEAN PESTO

MAKES ABOUT 1 CUP

THIS RECIPE WAS CREATED TO GO WITH the Red, White, and Green Vegetable "Lasagne" (page 163), but it can be used just as you would any pesto—in omelets, tossed with pasta, or as a savory dip.

¹/₄ pound green beans

1 teaspoon roughly chopped garlic (about 1 to 2 cloves)

¹/₂ teaspoon kosher salt

Freshly ground black pepper to taste

¹/₂ cup neutral-flavored cooking oil, such as canola or soybean

¹/₃ cup roasted pumpkin seeds

Blanch the green beans in boiling salted water for 1¹/₂ minutes. Remove them to an ice bath and then drain them in a colander.

Transfer the beans to the bowl of a food processor and add the garlic, salt, and pepper. Puree for 30 seconds and add half the oil while the motor is running. Add the pumpkin seeds and the remaining oil and process for 10 to 15 seconds, until smooth.

MAKE AHEAD The pesto can be refrigerated in an airtight container for up to 5 days.

PARSNIP-HERB BISCUITS

MAKES 15 2-INCH BISCUITS

USING ROASTED PARSNIP PUREE as a base and adding a few fresh herbs results in rich but still light and flavorful biscuits.

9 tablespoons (1 stick plus 1 tablespoon)
  cold unsalted butter

1 leek, thinly sliced

$1^{1}/_{2}$ cups all-purpose flour

$^{1}/_{2}$ cup yellow cornmeal

2 tablespoons sugar

$2^{1}/_{2}$ teaspoons baking powder

$^{3}/_{4}$ teaspoon kosher salt

$^{1}/_{2}$ teaspoon baking soda

4 ounces semihard cheese (page 23),
  grated (1 cup)

2 ounces Parmesan or other hard cheese
  (page 23), roughly chopped ($^{1}/_{2}$ cup)

2 tablespoons fresh thyme

$1^{1}/_{2}$ teaspoons freshly ground black
  pepper

$1^{1}/_{2}$ cups Roasted Parsnip Puree
  ($^{1}/_{2}$ recipe; page 152)

2 large eggs

$1^{1}/_{2}$ tablespoons apple cider vinegar

$^{1}/_{4}$ cup milk

In a medium skillet over medium heat, melt 1 tablespoon of the butter. Add the leek and sauté for 2 minutes. Remove from the heat and set aside to cool.

Preheat the oven to 425°F.

In a food processor, pulse the flour, cornmeal, sugar, baking powder, salt, and baking soda until combined. Add the remaining 8 tablespoons butter and pulse until the pieces are the size of fine bread crumbs.

Transfer the mixture to a large bowl. Stir in the cheeses, thyme, and pepper. In a separate bowl, mix together the parsnip puree, eggs, vinegar, and milk. Stir in the leek. Add the parsnip mixture to the cheese mixture and mix until evenly moistened. Turn the dough out onto a generously floured surface. Knead gently until the dough just holds together, about 10 turns. Sprinkle the work surface again with flour and pat the dough into a $1^{1}/_{4}$-inch-thick rectangle.

Cut the dough into rounds with a floured biscuit cutter or drinking glass 2 to $2^{1}/_{2}$ inches in diameter. Transfer to two ungreased baking sheets, leaving 2 inches of space between each biscuit. Bake the biscuits for 7 minutes and then rotate the pans in the oven. Bake for an additional 8 to 10 minutes, or until golden brown.

Let the biscuits rest for 5 minutes before serving.

MAKE AHEAD These biscuits taste best the day they are made, but they will keep for 2 to 3 days in an airtight container at room temperature. They can also be frozen for up to 1 month. Reheat in the oven before serving.

SOURCES

MARKETS, FOOD SHOPS, AND RESTAURANTS

Community Supported Agriculture (CSA)
To find a CSA in your area, go to Local Harvest, an information resource that connects consumers with small farmers.
www.localharvest.org/csa/

Farmer's Markets
Two helpful websites can guide you to a USDA-certified market near you:
http://farmersmarket.com *and*
http://www.ams.usda.gov, *the Agricultural Marketing Service of the USDA.*

Bennett's Pure Food Bistro
7650 SE 27th Street, #100
Mercer Island, WA 98040
(206) 232-2759
www.bennettsbistro.com

Pasta & Co
Four locations in the Seattle, Washington, area
www.pastaco.com

Pike Place Market
Year-round open market offering fresh produce, meats, seafood, and artisanal products.
Pike Place and First Avenue
Seattle, WA 98101
www.pikeplacemarket.org

Tom Douglas Restaurants
Seattle-based restaurateur and chef with four restaurants in the Seattle area, including Dahlia Lounge and Bakery, The Palace Kitchen, Etta's Seafood, and Lola.
(206) 448-2001
www.tomdouglas.com

MEAT AND SEAFOOD

City Fish
The longest-running fish market in Seattle's Pike Place Market, this seafood company sells everything from fresh salmon to Dungeness crab. They will ship anywhere.
1535 Pike Place
Pike Place Market
Seattle, WA 98101
(800) 334-2669
www.cityfish.com

EatWild.com
A website source listing information on grass-fed meat, including where to purchase it in your area.
http://eatwild.com

Isernio's
A Seattle-based sausage company producing all-natural sausages.
5600 Seventh Avenue South
Seattle, WA 98108
(206) 762-6207 or 1 (888) 495-8674
www.isernio.com

FRUITS AND VEGETABLES

Chukar Cherries
A Washington State fruit company specializing in dried fruits and jams.
1529B Pike Place
Pike Place Market
Seattle, WA 98101
(800) 624-9544
www.chukar.com

Mike and Jean's Berry Farm
A socially and environmentally responsible Washington State farm specializing in strawberries and raspberries.
16502 Jungquist Road
Mt. Vernon, WA 98273
(360) 424-7220
www.mikeandjeans.com

Gingerich Farms Products, Inc.
An Oregon farm that sells dehydrated blueberries, hazelnuts, and other Pacific Northwest food products.
PO Box 910
Canby, OR 97013
(877) 857-5816 or (503) 651-3742
www.gingerich.com

Tiny's Organic
A Washington State family farm that sells fruits, vegetables, and gift baskets. It ships nationwide and provides local delivery in the Seattle metropolitan area.
(866) 358-TINY or (206) 762-0577
www.ilovetiny.com

ARTISANAL CHEESE

Beecher's Handmade Cheese
1600 Pike Place
Pike Place Market
Seattle, WA 98101
(206) 956-1964
www.beechershandmadecheese.com

Grafton Village Cheese Company
A Vermont cheese company specializing in cow's-milk Cheddars. They also sell maple syrup.
PO Box 87
Grafton, VT 05146
(800) 472-3866
www.graftonvillagecheese.com

Juniper Grove Farms
A farmstead cheese producer from Oregon known for goat's-milk Tumalo Tomme.
2024 SW Fifty-eighth Street
Redmond, OR 97756
(541) 923-8353

Marin French Cheese Company

A California cheese company specializing in two handmade French-style cheeses, Camembert and Brie, as well as fresh cheeses.

7500 Red Hill Road
Petaluma, CA 94952
(800) 292-6001
www.marinfrenchcheese.com

Maytag Dairy Farms

An Iowa dairy famous for blue cheese; they also produce Swiss, Cheddar, and Edam.

2282 E. Eighth Street N
Newton, IA 50208
(800) 247-2458
www.maytagdairyfarms.com

Mozzarella Company

Texas cheesemaker Paula Lambert (a.k.a. the best-dressed woman in the cheese business) specializes in cow's- and goat's-milk cheeses.

2944 Elm Street
Dallas, TX 75226
(214) 741-4072 or (800) 798-2954
www.mozzco.com

Oregon Gourmet Cheeses

An Oregon cheese company specializing in cow's-milk cheeses.

815 First Avenue E
Albany, OR 97321
(541) 928-8888
www.oregongourmetcheeses.com

Pleasant Valley Dairy

A small Washington State cheese company producing cow's-milk cheeses; known for Gouda.

6804 Kickerville Road
Ferndale, WA 98248
(360) 366-5398

Point Reyes Farmstead Cheese Company

A family-owned California cheese company specializing in blue cheese.

PO Box 9
Point Reyes Station, CA 94956
(800) 591-6878
www.pointreyescheese.com

The Rogue Creamery

Oregon cheese company producing cow's-milk blue cheeses.

PO Box 3606
Central Point, OR 97502
(541) 665-1155 or (866) 665-1155
www.roguecreamery.com

Sally Jackson Cheeses

A small Washington State producer of cow's-, sheep's-, and goat's-milk cheeses.

16 Nealy Road
Oroville, WA 98844
www.sallyjacksoncheeses.com

Sierra Nevada Cheese Company

A small California cheese company specializing in cow's-milk Jack cheese and cream cheese.

6505 Country Road 39
Willows, CA 95988
(530) 934-8660
www.sierranevadacheese.com

Vella Cheese Company

Cheese pioneer Ig Vella's California cheese company produces cow's-milk Jack, Cheddar, and Italian-style cheeses.

315 Second Street East
Sonoma, CA 95476
(707) 938-3232 or (800) 848-0505
www.vellacheese.com

Willamette Valley Cheese Company

Oregon cheesemaker producing cow's- and sheep's-milk cheeses.

8105 Wallace Avenue NW
Salem, OR 97304
(503) 399-9806
www.wvcheeseco.com

ARTISANAL BREAD

Grand Central Bakery

An artisanal bread company with locations in Seattle, Washington, and Portland, Oregon.

Seattle: (206) 768-0320
Portland: (503) 232-0575
www.grandcentralbakery.com

HANDCRAFTED BEER AND WINE

Domaine Drouhin Oregon

A winery in Oregon's Willamette Valley producing Pinot Noir and Chardonnay.

PO Box 700
Dundee, OR 97115
(503) 864-2700
www.domainedrouhin.com

Redhook Ale Brewery

Washington State–based microbrewery.

Woodinville Brewery
14300 NE 145th Street
Woodinville, WA 98072
(425) 483-3232
www.redhook.com

Quilceda Creek Vintners

Washington state winery in the Yakima Valley producing Cabernet Sauvignon.

PO Box 1562
Snohomish, WA 98291
(360) 568-2389
www.quilcedacreek.com

NATURAL FOODS COMPANY

Pacific Natural Foods

Producers of pure foods, including soups, stocks, and beverages.

19480 SW Ninety-seventh Avenue
Tualatin, OR 97062
(503) 692-9666
www.pacificfoods.com

ACKNOWLEDGMENTS

Top thanks to longtime cooking "wing-man" Lura Smith; all of the tasters and testers; and to everyone at Beecher's, Bennett's, and Pasta & Co, practically all of whom had input and influenced the recipes in this book.

And of course you wouldn't be reading this book without The Gourmet Grrl, Laura Holmes Haddad, my collaborator; Julie Riendl, our project warden; Carole Bidnick, our agent; and the operator of my life, my assistant, Erica Wiley Pisconski.

Big thanks to the Clarkson Potter team: my editor, Rica Allannic, as well as Jane Treuhaft and Kathleen Fleury. For the stunning photography, I have to thank Maren Caruso and Scott Mansfield and food stylists Kim Konecny and Julia Scahill.